The Erotic Contemplative

Michael Bernard Kelly was born in Melbourne in 1954. He held professional qualifications in theology, spirituality, education and creative media. For seventeen years he was employed as a Religious Education specialist in the Catholic education system. In 1993 he came out as an openly gay man, and his career in Catholic education ended. Michael then committed himself to living contemplatively and to shaping new forms of ministry with gay and lesbian people. He was a freelance writer, speaker, activist, counsellor, and educator, specialising in spirituality, sexuality, and human integration. His ministry included creating rituals, speaking at conferences, leading retreats, offering spiritual direction, and writing for journals, newspapers and books in Australia, the US and the UK. Michael died in November 2020.

Michael was an Adjunct Research Associate at Monash University's Centre for Religious Studies, Australia. He is the author/presenter of *The Erotic Contemplative* video-lecture series (Erospirit Research Institute, 1995) and accompanying *Study Guide* released to coincide with the relaunch of the videos (Clouds of Magellan Press, 2020); author of *Seduced by Grace: Contemporary Spirituality, Gay Experience and Christian Faith* (Clouds of Magellan Press, 2007, 2021); and, based on his 2015 PhD, *Christian Mysticism's Queer Flame: Spirituality in the Lives of Contemporary Gay Men* (Routledge Studies in Religion, 2019).

The Erotic Contemplative

Reflections on the Spiritual Journey of the Gay/Lesbian Christian

*

MICHAEL BERNARD KELLY

Clouds of Magellan Press | Melbourne

© 2021, Joseph Kramer, Erospirit Research Institute and The Estate of Michael Bernard Kelly

All rights reserved

ISBN: 978-0-6451935-7-2

Published 2021 by Clouds of Magellan Press, Melbourne, Australia.

www.cloudsofmagellanpress.net

Contents

Publisher's Note and Acknowledgements — vii

Foreword—Joseph Kramer — ix

Introduction—Michael Bernard Kelly — xiii

A Note on Language — xvii

1. The Truth of Our Experience — *1*

    Study Guide — *30*

2. Re-visioning Sexuality and Spirituality — *33*

    Study Guide — *64*

3. Exodus and Awakening — *67*

    Study Guide — *94*

4. The Desert and the Dark — *99*

    Study Guide — *131*

5. Liberation — *137*

    Study Guide — *167*

6. The Road From Emmaus — *171*

    Study Guide — *195*

Publisher's Note and Acknowledgements

This book is a transcription of *The Erotic Contemplative* lectures by Michael Bernard Kelly, recorded in 1994 under the auspices of Dr Joseph Kramer and the Erospirit Research Institute, released as a six-part video series (1995), and re-released in 2020. Michael also wrote a study guide to accompany the re-release. That guide and Michael's general introduction to the lecture series have been incorporated into this book.

Dr Joseph Kramer of Erospirit graciously allowed us to publish this transcript in book form, and I thank him for his generosity, insight, and friendship. Joseph has also written a foreword about his first meeting with Michael and the genesis of the lectures. Carol Leigh from Erospirit, who filmed and edited the original video series, facilitated the transcription of the videos. These transcripts were checked against the lectures and edited by Helen Bell, who edited Michael's first book, *Seduced by Grace* (Clouds of Magellan Press 2007, 2021). I would like to mention that Helen also later transcribed many of the interviews Michael undertook for his PhD, as well as providing editing of the PhD, published later by Routledge as *Christian Mysticism's Queer Flame: Spirituality in the Lives of Contemporary Gay Men* (2019).

In editing the lectures for print publication, we have applied a light touch. A few words have been added here and there to help sentences along, and a few words deleted for the same reason. 'Filler' phrases—such as 'in a sense'—have been pruned; but the text is essentially how Michael presented it in the talks. We have not corrected some of the instances of gendered language that place the talks in their time-space of 1994. Michael does comment on this in his 'A Note on Language' (p. xvii) below. Paragraph breaks have been added to render the text more accessible to the eye, though there are still some long paragraphs by normal layout standards. We chose not to break the text with subheadings, keeping that aspect of 'conversational and informal, rather than academic and formal' that Michael remarks on in his Introduction.

The result then, we hope is a lively encounter with Michael's thoughts and ideas—capturing 'the joy as it flies' (in the words of William Blake, a favourite quote of Michael's, which was one of the early title options for what became *Seduced by Grace*). But Michael's ideas are also here to be savoured slowly, and we hope these lectures, now in book form, receive many readings.

Thankyou also to Noelene Kelly for additional editing, Maria Pallotta-Chiarolli, Andrew Brown, Petrina Barson, Andrew Farrell and Marcus O'Donnell.

Gordon Thompson,
Publisher, Clouds of Magellan Press
November 2021

Foreword—Joseph Kramer

I first encountered Michael Kelly on the 6th of May 1993 at Newman Hall, Holy Ghost parish at the University of California at Berkeley. I had been invited to speak at the monthly gathering of the gay Catholic men's group. My topic for the evening was 'Gay Communal Living and Service'. I made sure my presentation included descriptions of several erotic rituals that could be practiced in a gay men's spiritual community. I also spoke of communal erotic states as prayer and as nourishment to support our lives of service.

After the talk, a man with an Australian accent introduced himself to me and invited me for coffee at Café Roma down the street. While we were sitting in Roma, I noticed how embodied Michael was, but not like a yoga instructor or athlete. It was how he spoke. His words seemed to exude from deep within his body. I was entranced. Michael asked me if I knew who Dominic Savio was. Of course, I did. He told me, 'Today is the feast of Dominic Savio, a day special to me as a Christian and as a gay man.' As he told me this, the theme from the movie *The Mission* began to play in the coffeehouse. I had played this very piece in over 100 erotic massage classes I had taught for gay men in the last five years. For me, this piece of music represented my commitment to service. This encounter at Roma is how my friendship with Michael Kelly began.

My day job was director of Erospirit Research Institute, which was dedicated to the integration of spirituality and sexuality during the horrific AIDS epidemic. Because there was no cure and fear about sex was everywhere, Erospirit was sponsoring a series of video talks for men called Gay Sex Wisdom. These were one-hour video 'podcasts' from queer visionaries long before podcasts were invented.

The first erotic-spiritual visionary I invited to present was Jim Mitulski, the pastor at the Metropolitan Community Church in the Castro in San Francisco. Jim had ministered to hundreds of mostly young men dying of AIDS and had officiated at more AIDS funerals than any clergyman in America. Other men who recorded *Gay Sex Wisdom* presentations included a Jewish mystic, a pagan, a Native American shaman, an ex-Jesuit, a sexworker and several sex radicals.

My contribution to the *Gay Sex Wisdom* series was *Sex Monasteries—An Invitation to Erotic Community*, based on the talk I had given the night I met Michael. After recording my talk, I sent Michael a copy with an invitation for him to contribute to the series. We met again at Café Roma to discuss his presentation. He planned to describe the mystical path that he saw available to gay and lesbian Christians. I reminded him that although the series was geared toward sexually-expressive gay men, his gender-inclusive mystical journey would be welcomed. He said he needed a few weeks to prepare his presentation.

At the beginning of September 1994, I was preparing to travel to Europe for several weeks of teaching. Michael volunteered to house sit for me. We arranged that while I was gone, Carol Leigh, my video artist, would come to my home and record his hour-long *Gay Sex Wisdom* presentation.

When I returned home from Europe, Michael told me the recording went quite well. The next day, I spoke to Carol who expressed surprise at how many video sessions it took to record Michael's presentation—six sessions of 90 minutes each! I was flabbergasted, and I became angry. I couldn't fathom how nine hours of Christian mysticism would fit into the *Gay Sex Wisdom* series. Then I watched Michael's presentation. My anger turned into surprise and then awe. His powerful words describing the path of *The Erotic Contemplative* seemed to come straight from his heart and right into mine.

I told Michael that he was offering transformative guidance, like Joseph Campbell did in his Hero's Journey. I said, 'You have described the Mystic's Journey for Gay and Lesbian Christians.' But I had no idea how to market his presentation. At first, I tried promoting it along with the *Gay Sex Wisdom* series and my erotic massage videos, but I only managed to sell six copies in six months.

I then got the idea of advertising in the *National Catholic Reporter*, one of the most liberal Catholic papers in the US. The response was amazing. Hundreds of orders began pouring in by mail. Apparently, many gay men and lesbians read the *National Catholic Reporter*.

Michael and I were both surprised that *The Erotic Contemplative* was finding its way into so many churches, schools and other religious establishments. Several spiritual directors from Catholic seminaries purchased *The Erotic Contemplative*. One college professor called me, telling me how moved the students in his class on pastoral counselling of sexual minorities were. At least six psychotherapists ordered *The Erotic Contemplative*. Dozens of orders came from Catholic parishes, where I imagined significant numbers of gay and lesbian parishioners.

I was most surprised by how many requests for *The Erotic Contemplative* came from Catholic monasteries. I remember the joy I felt receiving the first order from a Trappist monastery. Thomas Merton, also a Trappist, had been a major influence on my spirituality. In the coming months, I sent *The Erotic Contemplative* to more than twenty-five Catholic monasteries. I remember one monk writing that he had never seen the words 'erotic' and 'contemplative' used together, but he somehow felt them together within his body.

In one of his annual 6th of May emails to me, Michael wrote me, 'I am so grateful that *The Erotic Contemplative* has found its way into the hands and hearts of so many gay men and lesbians.'

Joseph Kramer, Ph.D.

Introduction

Michael Kelly's introduction from the Study Guide (Clouds of Magellan Press, 2019) *on the re-release of* The Erotic Contemplative *video series.*

In 1994 Dr Joseph Kramer of Erospirit Research Institute in California asked me if I would record some reflections that might support and encourage gay and lesbian Christians in reclaiming and re-imagining their spiritual lives (see 'A Note on Language' below). I was honoured by the invitation and excited by the project. These six lectures were my response to that invitation. They were recorded live in Oakland, California, in September and October, 1994, and published in both video and audiotape formats the next year.

The series was well-received, and for many years it circulated in these formats and was viewed and reflected upon by people all around the world. Over the decades, as often happens, the series gradually faded from view as new theologies, new voices and new technologies emerged, bringing both new insights and new forms of information sharing. Every so often, however, someone would contact me asking about *The Erotic Contemplative*, and inquiring about how they could access a copy of the series. As time went on such access became more and more problematic, as both video and audiotape formats became obsolete.

Eventually I realised that I was faced with a choice: I could allow the series to become increasingly inaccessible, or I could explore options for digitising the lectures. With the kind encouragement of Dr Joseph Kramer, who still had the original master copies of the tapes, the financial assistance of Mr Sean Crellin, and the technical help of Dr John Rolley, I decided to have the lectures professionally digitised and make them freely available online.

In re-releasing these lectures I have faced a number of issues.

Twenty-five years have passed since the initial recordings. Are they still relevant? Have developments in society, in the church, in theology, spirituality and biblical studies, and in LGBTIQ+ experience, moved on so far and so fast that these lectures no longer have much to offer? Are they talking about a time that has, thankfully, given way to a more enlightened and liberated present?

In personally revisiting and reviewing each of these lectures I have discovered several things. Firstly, many ideas and insights that were, arguably, groundbreaking and visionary twenty-five years ago are now relatively commonplace and unremarkable. In 1994, for example, it was still somewhat daring to suggest that gay relationships could not only be 'ok', but holy, filled with grace, sacraments of divine love, and gifts to the church and the world. Such an idea is now, thankfully, unremarkable in many church circles and communities—though it is very far from being universally accepted. The clearest manifestation of this kind of change is the fact that today same-sex marriage is legal in many countries, and these relationships are being blessed publicly by more and more churches. This was virtually unimaginable in 1994. Coming Out in 1994, to use another example, was far more challenging and potentially problematic than it is in 2019, at least in most progressive democratic countries.

At the same time, much in these lectures remains relevant and even, I hope, important. It surprises me, for example, that since recording the lectures, no-one else has really attempted to do what I aim to do in these tapes—which is to reframe and reimagine the traditional Christian mystical path in the context of the lives of self-affirming, fully open, sexually expressive queer people of faith.

In 2015 I graduated from a doctoral program at Monash University in Melbourne, Australia. During my studies I surveyed, in depth, the developments in queer theology, gay spirituality and allied fields (such as gender and religion) over the past forty years. I also considered emerging thought in the fields of Christian mysticism, faith development theory, and spiritual direction. While there has been a good deal of brilliant, visionary and even paradigm-shifting work in these fields, still no one has attempted the task I set myself back in 1994, when I was asked to record a few talks.

These lectures, then, still have some relevance and, I trust, they may still be of help to people who are seeking to integrate their lived sexuality with their call to mystical prayer and inner transformation. Of course, some parts of this eight-hour long course are somewhat dated—for example, there are some quite specific references to social and political events and issues that were clearly pressing at the time, but that are now simply part of twentieth century history.

A significant aspect of the lectures is that they were developed during a period when HIV/AIDS was still devastating the queer community. At the time there were few medications but there was a great deal of fear, rejection and prejudice; life expectancy for most people who contracted the virus was relatively short. The talks were recorded in the San Francisco Bay area, where I had been living for four years, and so, like the groundbreaking work of Dr Joseph Kramer, they emerged from a city and a community that were living through deep trauma that challenged every hope, every dream, every possibility, every relationship, every individual and every community of faith. This was also a time when many churches were still refusing not only to minister to people living with HIV, but even to bury the bodies of the dead. We now know that there were many priests and ministers of religion whose death certificates were altered so that AIDS was not mentioned, such was the shame, such was the rejection. There were some shining examples of true Christian love, like the ministry at Most Holy Redeemer, a Catholic parish in the Castro, but these were fairly rare.

In such a climate, it is not surprising that most gay/queer theology or spirituality of the period was developed against the backdrop of repression, exclusion and condemnation. New approaches to scripture, moral theology, and church history were being explored, but overwhelmingly these were shaped as an argument against the oppression of queer people. Such arguments were, and sadly still are, essential. However, arguing that queer people can live fully self-affirming, sexually expressive lives as Christians is not the same as exploring how such lives might be lived—or, indeed, how they actually are being lived. Nor do such arguments offer wisdom around the spiritual patterns and movements that might emerge in such lives, and how these might be understood in light of the rich history of Christian spirituality and mysticism. Beyond even this lies the question of how such lives might challenge and potentially transform the spiritual and mystical tradition itself.

This was what I set out to explore in these lectures, and to my knowledge, and twenty-five years on, no one else has attempted to do this. My recent doctoral work, which takes this exploration to a new level and brings it into academic theological discourse, is significant precisely because of this persistent lack within the overall fields of both queer theology and Christian spirituality.

It is in this context that I decided to consider re-releasing these video-lectures, despite the fact that they are, perhaps, somewhat dated. I was also persuaded by friends and colleagues who insisted that the material remains important, and that the approach taken in these talks, which is conversational and informal rather than academic and formal, makes them accessible and engaging. My hope is that these lectures will genuinely be, as the original flyer for the series suggested, a 'stimulus for living, loving and prayer'.

Welcome, friend, to *The Erotic Contemplative*.

Michael Bernard Kelly PhD

August 6, 2019
Feast of the Transfiguration
Melbourne, Australia

A Note on Language

I have kept the original title of the series as it appears on each video-lecture. In 1994 it was fairly bold to include 'gay and lesbian' in a title like this. In the early 1990s the term queer was just beginning to be reclaimed and used as a daring and confronting term that included all genders—but this was by no means universally accepted. For many people who identified as gay or lesbian, the word 'queer' was still a slur, still offensive. Later terms like LGBTIQ+ were quite unknown at the time these lectures were developed. Terms such as 'cis-gender' were still far in the future. Were I recording these lectures today, in 2019, I would have included such terms, and I offer my sincere apology to any listeners who may feel excluded or alienated by my use of 'gay and lesbian'. My clear intention in the lectures was to use language that was as inclusive as possible—but, like everyone else, I was a person of my times.

In the lectures I also make it clear that I am speaking as a 'man' (we would now say a 'cis-gender man') who identifies as 'gay', and that I can only credibly speak from my own perspective and experience. I was initially reluctant, therefore, to include 'lesbian' in the title. However, in reviewing and editing the series Dr Kramer stressed that he felt my language throughout was so inclusive, and that the material itself was so broadly helpful, that we should make the title as inclusive as possible. MBK

1

The Truth of our Experience

A warm welcome to this journey, this extraordinary journey of integrating Christian contemplative experience with the gay journey, the gay sexual experience. And I'm aware that as I begin to talk, although we're separated by time and space, we truly are not separate. Because in spirit, there's no separation, there's no time and space, there's no division. As Thomas Merton said, in the last talk he gave before he died, 'Brothers, we are already one, we only imagine that we are not.' So let's take a moment to be silent and to be still, so that we may really be in our hearts, that what I speak may be from my heart, and perhaps in some sense from the heart of God. And that it may also speak to your heart where you are in your place, in your time, in your life's journey. So let's be silent together.

*

I'm aware, in the silence, of our ancestors, of all those gay men and women, down through the centuries of Christian history, who've lived and loved other gay men, other gay women. And they've lived and loved their journeys in company with Christ, many of whom have suffered and died for those loves. We pray that their spirit may be with us and may guide us and enlighten and enliven us.

*

In Scripture, it says that no word of God goes forth and returns to God empty without accomplishing what that word was sent for. So my prayer is also that these simple poor words that I offer you may in some sense carry something of that word of the Divine, and that it may go forth into your heart and your life and achieve and accomplish what it was sent for. Which may not be my plan and may not be your plan, but which is the plan of the Divine lover, to draw us deeper into the Divine embrace in every step we take in our lives.

This journey of the gay contemplative life is an extraordinary one, and one that in many ways has never been fully explored or fully talked about. Firstly, when I use the word 'gay' I'm talking primarily in these tapes to gay men. I'm a gay man. I'm not a gay woman. I'm not a lesbian woman. I can't speak for women, nor can I speak for heterosexual men. Hopefully some heterosexual men and women and some lesbian women will listen in and draw from these tapes what is good for them, and you are most welcome. But primarily what I say will come from the life experience of a gay man and be directed to the life experiences of other gay men, men who primarily, not solely, but primarily find their affectionate fullness, their life companionship and their major sexual delight in loving other men.

When I speak of Christian, I'm not speaking of people who are fully paid-up card-carrying members of the Catholic club or of any other Christian denominational club. I'm not speaking necessarily of people who buy or accept or subscribe to all of the doctrines, and all of the teachings and all of the history of Christianity. The people I am speaking to, what I am speaking of, are those who find in the story of Christ, in the words of Scripture, in Christian heritage, a model, a pattern, a guide, a myth, a great story, which can inform our lives and our hearts, our living and our loving. I'm also, I suppose, speaking to people who have a particular commitment and devotion to Jesus, to the Christ, in the many different ways we image him, including those who image Christ as Christa, or Sophia, the Divine Wisdom, so that the feminine principle is also included in our love for Christ.

And when I speak of 'contemplative', a more difficult word, what I'm speaking about is a certain way of being spiritual, a certain way of living a Christian life, which has its roots in silence, in the experience of the desert, an experience of emptiness, of dryness, of quiet, of peace within. I'm certainly not speaking primarily from the activist mode. You know, most of Christianity in recent centuries has been extremely active, and a lot of our spiritualities have centered around simply actively loving other people, which of course is always at the heart of the Christian journey. But sometimes it's spoken about as if that's it.

The contemplative journey is really about the inner life, the life hidden with God in Christ, as we say, often hidden from oneself in many senses, a life of trust, a life of openness, a life of stillness. It's the life that, in terms of its historical incarnation, often in the desert or in monasteries, not a lot of people are called to. But it's also the life that really is the wellspring and the heart of Christian spirituality. Time and time again, through Christian centuries, you find that it's the contemplatives that people turn to, to develop this sense of what it means to be spiritual, what it means to be Christian. And this tradition, which is really at the heart of Christianity, in many ways has been lost in recent times in the very activist, very outgoing, externally oriented West. It's still very much present in the Eastern Orthodox churches, and certainly in pockets in the West. But we tend to have lost a lot of this wisdom, so that people turn to the Eastern religions, thinking that there is no contemplative tradition, no mystical tradition within Christianity. And here, I'm not talking about the so-called esoteric Christianity, which draws from gnostic texts, some genuine and some spurious. I am talking about the mainstream, deep Christian tradition of mysticism, which is present in all the writings and is available for everyone.

I would hope that this journey we take together in these tapes may, if nothing else, be partly a recovery of some of that profound tradition. I note that Thomas Merton again, when he visited the

Dalai Lama and many of the High Lamas around him in Dharamsala, came away saying that in his conversations (and by the way Thomas Merton was a great admirer of Buddhism), the Lamas and he ended up agreeing that everything they had, was also in Christianity. But then Thomas Merton was a contemplative *par excellence*. He knew the tradition deeply and it's only when we go deeply into the tradition that we find this profound contemplative wisdom. That's what we hope to do in these tapes.

So, having said all those disclaimers, and setting out that geography, let's begin.

There's a wonderful poem at the beginning of a book by MC Richards, a book called *Centering*. It's by a man called John Middleton Murray, and I think it should be printed on a holy card and given to every Christian at baptism. It goes like this: 'For the good man, the good person, to realize that it is better to be whole than to be good is to enter on a straight and narrow path, compared to which his previous rectitude was flowery license.' To be whole, rather than good. And I note that those words 'straight and narrow path' come from scripture where Jesus says that the road to life is straight and narrow and few enter on it. And I think implicit in the poem is the idea that the road to wholeness rather than goodness (as it's commonly understood, even within a lot of Christian teaching, and certainly within the society as a whole; witness, you know, the Moral Majority for example) is a journey, a road that few people really enter on. It asks everything of us, and it will challenge everything within us and transform us totally. No wonder that few people enter on it. But it is the road of the contemplative journey.

As we begin this journey, I'm also conscious that there will be some people who are asking, why bother with Christianity? Christianity has been so much associated especially with the oppression of gay people, including today. This is not something that has necessarily dramatically changed, especially in the US. For a lot of gay people, it's painful to even hear the word 'Christian', and certainly to consider the idea that one could find in Christianity a path to wholeness of life as a gay person.

I'd like to tell you a story. A few years ago, when I was living in the US, it was Christmas time. And it was winter here. I come from Australia, as you may have gathered. In Australia, of course, it was high summer. And it was Christmas Eve, and it was cold, and I was feeling very alone, very lonely, very despondent. Thinking about my family, at the same time thinking about a lot of family stuff, as we tend to do at Christmas time, a lot of family pain and dysfunction that we all share. Christmases past coming to mind. I was also aware of pain within the Christian tradition, of the beauty of Christmas and the message of God becoming human, the vulnerability of the little child, the intimacy of Mary and Joseph in the stable, but all the trips that Christianity has laid on us down through the centuries. And while I was reflecting on this, I got a phone call from 8000 miles away across the Pacific. And it was my younger sister who I'm very close to. And while we were chatting, she said, 'I'd like to play you something'. And she played for me over the phone, a piece of music, which I would love to play for you but legalities preclude that unfortunately. It was something I'd never heard. It was the Irish singer Enya. And what she was singing was not something from *Watermark* or something familiar. It was 'Silent Night'. And she was singing it in Gaelic. Gaelic is the ancient Irish language, which was largely stamped out during the penal days, during the days of persecution, in an attempt to squash the Irish and to squash the Catholic religion in Ireland. It's also a language that goes back to pre-Christian times, so it dates before the advent of Christianity with its own persecution of the Celtic religion. Somehow when I heard that music in Gaelic (by the way, my ancestors are Irish and our family has a fairly strong Irish flavor to it, especially my mother), it was as if I was hearing my family language, from before all the pain, from before the dysfunction, from before the particularities of the mess that I inherited within my own family. And somehow this language, which

I didn't fully understand, reached through the centuries, from my ancestors to me in that moment, my true family, my true heritage, and touched me. At the same time, I was hearing 'Silent Night'. And it felt the same with Christianity, as if the pure and simple story of God becoming human, to love us more deeply, to draw us into God's love—as if that simple story reached across all the centuries of pain and persecution, of the burning of gay people, of the death of so many women. And that pure story touched me as well, in that moment, brought to me by the love of my sister, by a real physical human being who I love and who loves me. And this pure note, sounding literally across 8000 miles of the dark Pacific, was like a pure note of my true tradition, sounding through the centuries to touch my heart.

My prayer is that in all that we say in these tapes, the pure note of Christian tradition, the pure note of truth, the pure note of deep spiritual life, which is for all, and especially for those most oppressed, most rejected, that that pure note will sound in your heart, you'll hear the language of your true family, you'll hear the true language of spiritual life.

So in this first session, what I want to do is to lay down some fundamental principles of the spiritual life, and of integrating the gay experience with the spiritual life in the Christian tradition. I also want to offer some notes for spiritual directors. In the Christian tradition, we have an ancient heritage of looking for spiritual guides or mentors who are not gurus as in the Hindu tradition, but someone who has walked the journey before us, perhaps more deeply than us, and can be a mentor, can listen to us and our story, and listen for that pure note within our story, and reveal it to ourselves, help us to attune our ears and our hearts to hear it. So this is also for spiritual directors as well.

This journey that we're going to take is fundamentally a journey from slavery to freedom, to the glorious freedom of the children of God, which is the heritage of every human being. A journey from oppression and persecution, to liberation, from death to new life. And, of course, the great model of all Christian life is the death and resurrection of Jesus. From fragmentation to full union within, from brokenness to wholeness, from being asleep to being fully awake, from being half alive to being alive. It's truly a liberation theology, a liberation spirituality, as all true spiritualities must be. If they bind, if they enslave, they are no true spirituality, whatever tradition they come from.

This term liberation theology, or liberation spirituality, as many of us are aware, arose in Latin America in the last few decades from people who had been oppressed for centuries, oppressed economically, oppressed in terms of their land, oppressed in terms of their self-image, and who had also experienced religion as something which, although it spoke to them in their own lives, was also used as a tool of their oppression. And so some of the wisdom that we will look at comes from them, from those poor people, many of whom have died for the sake of this tradition, of this liberation, and continue to die, many of their deaths funded and supported covertly through this culture that we share in the West. I'm thinking of something Paul Monette said in his book, *Becoming a Man*, a wonderful line, where he simply said, 'Such obedient slaves we make with such very tidy rooms'.

The first step in liberation is to realize that we are in slavery, to see the truth of our situation, however painful it may be, to face the fact that we are in slavery. This can be the hardest for those who benefit most from the slavery. And so particularly, it can be difficult for white western men. Because if we keep our slavery hidden, if we obey the laws, if we are obedient slaves with tidy rooms, we can enjoy all the privileges of being white men in our culture. Now to wake up and see that as slavery is a great act of courage. It's also a great shock, and it's a great challenge. And we are the ones who can find it most difficult. As usual, it's the poor who are most inclined to take this journey, because the poor don't have much to lose. So blessed are the poor again and again, as Jesus said, because they have the courage to journey. It's our recognition that we are the poor and oppressed that allows us to go on this journey with them.

This is to enter the way of 'conscientization', which is the term used in Latin America, which also carries the sense of conscience, of learning what we have to do in our deepest heart, what our true core is. It's also something that was very real for the monks, the desert monks, in the first centuries of Christianity (we'll talk about them a little later), who formed the basis of a lot of Christian spirituality, and especially the contemplative tradition, that they woke up and realized they were in slavery in the societies in which they lived, and they left them. So this 'seeing', this 'becoming aware', is fundamental in the Christian spiritual tradition, and in gay life.

The second step is to believe that things could be different, to analyze the causes of our oppression and our slavery, to analyze them ruthlessly and honestly, and then to imagine the possibility of life being different for us. In doing this, and all that we do, we need to form communities. This is very hard to do and very hard to sustain, very hard to hold alone. We need to form communities of resistance, and communities of support, true communities that will discern together.

The next stage is to turn to Scripture, and to turn to the tradition, the tradition of spirituality, the tradition of Christian life that we share, and to find that it is our story. It is the story of the oppressed and the enslaved. It is not the story of the powerful. It's the story of the powerless. It's our story. As I say, this is also true of the spiritual literature, which fills 2000 years of Christian living, it's our story. And to really own this, we need very good exegesis; we need to break down the texts to discover what belongs to simply their cultural conditioning, and what are in fact the pure notes that can speak to us in our time and in our situation. So learning and true wisdom is very important in doing this. I'd like to compare this with the tradition of the monks. *Lectio Divina* is the bread and butter of the life of monks.

It's about reading scripture, not as an academic, but not without academic wisdom either. But you read it prayerfully and reflectively, and slowly, and when something touches your heart, you stop. And you stay with that, you go no further, and you sit in that. And you will allow that to fill your whole being, and to draw you into silent presence. And when it's time to move on, you take up the scripture again. This is the way we need to read Scripture. This is the way we need to find our story in it.

To do this, of course, as a gay man and a lesbian is to be very daring. We have been told that our stories are not in the Scripture, and that if they are they are only there in order to condemn us. So to take it up, and to really fully see it as speaking to us in our sexuality, not just in our so-called spiritual life, but in our sexual lives as well, is still quite daring for most Christians, for most people on any spiritual path, because sexuality and spirituality supposedly do not interweave, they oppose one another. In fact, the reverse is true.

The next stage, of course, is to act. The question, What then must we do? We've seen our slavery, we've formed communities of resistance and support, we've come to believe things could be different, we've analyzed our oppression, we've read the story and taken it into our hearts and seen it as speaking to us. We've dared to believe it could be our story. What do we do next? What is the call? What then? How must we move? Okay, what does this lead us to, both in overall direction for our lives and in very specific situations. In Latin America, this process is directed to very specific situations like a strike or a statement by the government or another example of oppression.

I think here of a group like Act Up, often looking at specific instances and saying, 'what do we do now?' or 'what do we do about this?' So there's also a need to move, not just to reflect. Now in all of this, part of the subtext is education. We can't do this just by sitting in a room and becoming spiritual. We also have to educate ourselves. And this is especially true for people who are involved in spiritual direction. Many gay men and lesbians will come to you really believing that the story of Christianity is one of oppression and slavery, and that they don't find their stories in Scripture and tradition. Now, if you're going to be a guide for them, or if you're not a spiritual director, if we're going to support one another, we have to be educated ourselves, both in true scriptural understandings, and in the life story of gay men and lesbians, so that we can become resources for one another, and no longer slaves to the version of our stories that has been handed to us. So education is really important. It's especially important because the church itself, the very body supposed to be the way to wholeness and holiness for people in Christianity is very often the one who does the worst oppressing. And to become free of that, very often we need someone else to speak those words of freedom to us. And that person has to have done their homework.

So if you're working with gay and lesbian people, educate yourself around conscientization, around what it means to be gay and lesbian and our experiences, and around what it can be to apply scripture to that journey of liberation. In doing this, whether we're guiding someone else or supporting each other, we have to be aware this is a very, very painful journey. It will shake us up in every moment of our lives. It will shake up all that we've ever believed about Christianity and about Christ, and especially about the church. It will shake up what we believe about ourselves. So there is a real need for gentleness, for patience, for a quiet leading with love and understanding and acceptance, for a word that liberates from guilt. Because as we start to break the molds we've been handed, start to violate the so-called laws we've been given, we feel the pain of this, we feel the danger of this, we feel 'out on a limb'. We feel fragile, we feel as if 'is this it, am I getting it, am I way off?' And we need words that can help us and reassure us that this is the way, trust the spirit within, trust your own wisdom.

This also can involve a certain kind of leaving of the church, which is very painful for someone who takes their life with Christ seriously. Now, in this leaving and all the coming out talk that I will use in these tapes, I don't essentially necessarily mean coming out in the full public sense. Although you know, to be honest, that is where my own tendencies lie. And I noticed recently a Zen master in San Francisco was saying you can't practice Zen unless you are fully out. Because you [otherwise] can't be true in the moment. And there's a certain sense to that. But of course, more important than coming out publicly is coming out within, coming out to God, if you like, coming out in our own spiritual lives. That's the true coming out, which either must precede or must follow or must accompany any other kind of coming out. And that's the more painful one, I believe. That is the more painful one, because it's us that is being shattered and remade. Our conditionings, our senses of self, not so much the world around us.

Many of us have given our lives to the church, have given our lives to Christ in the church, and to have our understandings of Christ and of the church broken and shattered is extremely painful. So we need to go slowly and gently and allow this to happen in its own time. And by the grace of the Spirit. It's not for us to take up the hammer and shatter the container. The container will break, but it will break because the fullness within is breaking us like a bird breaking an eggshell from within. The mother doesn't come up with a beak and break the shell, she allows the bird within, the Holy Spirit within, to break the container when the time is right. This is always God's initiative. This is not our doing, this is the work of the Holy Spirit. If it weren't, I would be very reluctant to invite anyone on this way because this way is so demanding, and it will shatter all that we are, all that we know of ourselves. It has to be the work of the Holy Spirit that leads us forward.

At the same time, there may be the need to speak a challenging word, not in anger or frustration but in truth. Sometimes the right word can be the gong sounding, can be the Zen master using the stick to wake up the pupil. But always this has to be discerned from within, and reluctantly. We don't speak the challenging word, the deeply challenging word, too readily, too quickly. This, of course, is very clear when coming out is involved, for coming out in a public sense can mean people's careers, people's families, even of course people's lives. And I really believe this has to be a movement of God within us. We can help one another and support one another and prepare the ground. But the final movement has to be God's, The costs are too great. They're too painful. It has to be a decision from the person within. And in some senses, I truly believe that God leaves us free in that moment; the spirit may lead us to that point but there's a freedom that we can make this choice or not. And I do believe that sooner or later we will make it if we are following the lead of the spirit. But always there's this respect for the integrity and the dignity and the freedom of the individual. And that must come from us as well as from God. In all of this, what we have to be doing is listening. And really this whole talk is about the truth of our experience.

Carter Hayward said the only theology that is worth anything at all is theology born in the crucible of experience, the truth. And if there's one thing that honest to God I could say to gay and lesbian people in the church, it is tell the truth, first to ourselves, and then to others, the truth of our experience. I'm tired of hearing other people tell us what we experience or how we should experience it. Theology and spirituality have traditionally been referred to as faith seeking understanding; great term, but we tend to think of faith as something in the head, you know, like a notional assent to doctrines and truths and formulations. That is not what faith is. Faith is the response of the whole person, body, mind, spirit and heart. That's what faith is. It's our whole life in every moment, in all our relating, including our sexual relating.

Now, that kind of faith seeking understanding, that's true theology. That is true spirituality. Some of the people who are so-called doing theology and doing spirituality, need to step back a couple of steps and live and let faith happen first, true faith in the body, in life. Then they can do theology. I wonder if this is why a lot of our theology seems so dead and so utterly irrelevant. And I speak as someone who studied theology for a number of years, so I have some sense of what I'm talking about. And after a while, you think, why bother? I mean, who really cares? Who is this speaking to? It has to come from lived experience and be a reflection on lived experience. And I think as gay and lesbian people, we can really offer some of these gifts to the church. Because anything that's going to do us any good in theology or spirituality will have to speak to our bodies and to the truth of our lives.

Now, here I come to a very crucial point in the whole series of tapes that we're going to go through together. And this is that our spiritual and our historical lives, our actual lives in history, are not separate. We do not have a so-called inner life and a so-called outer life, even though for the sake of talking, we have to sometimes use those terms and make distinctions. We live one life. We are one organism, one whole, one reality. And we can't buy into this splitting, this dualism, which says, 'Well, this is the way I am internally but you know, when I go to work, I can be completely different. When I go to church, I can be completely different.' Now, a lot of gay people have done this or have had to do this to survive. Well, folks, the time has passed, let's take some risks, let's lead the way a little, let's be on the edge. We so often have been in history, why not now when it's so deeply needed by so many people. Our historical and spiritual lives are one, our bodily lives, our spiritual lives are one. Someone said that in our lovemaking is the way we discover how we love God. These are not separate split-off bits of us. It's one.

Now a lot of spirituality (and this is a serious problem for someone who wants to mine the spiritual literature) is written as if the historical lives did not occur. It's a really serious problem. In fact, if you read the biographies of the people who wrote the stuff, a lot of the same things were happening in their historical lives as well. A classic example for me is John of the Cross, one of the great spiritual masters in the Christian tradition. In one of his most wonderful poems, he speaks about escaping on a dark night, by a secret ladder, where none saw him, and he goes out into the streets to pursue the beloved. This poem, in the Dark Night of the Soul, was written sometime after John had in fact escaped from a prison, where he had been persecuted and beaten and tortured by his own brothers in the Carmelite monastic order in 17th century Spain. He'd had a new jailer after several months of really painful treatment, inhuman treatment, and this guy was a little bit more human. He allowed John to have a needle and thread to sew his clothes, and John used the needle and thread to sew things together and made a ladder and escaped down out of the jail on a dark night, seen by no one. Later, this appears in John's poetry, in his then very developed analysis of that [escape] in relation to spiritual life, but it actually happened in history. It was in his actual life.

Teresa of Avila, another one of our great mystics, has a crucial life-turning moment when she reads the Confessions of St Augustine and recognizes herself there. When she sees an image of Christ crowned with thorns, suddenly her heart is split open and her whole life changes, and she begins to become the Teresa we know of. Now, when did this happen? When she turned 40. Midlife folks, midlife. She'd lived one kind of life, there was a seminal turning point and her life fell apart, and the second journey began. The true Teresa that we now know as Teresa of Avila, St Teresa of Avila. It's historical fact. It happened in her historical life, not just in her spirit.

We look at Therese Lisieux, a wonderful French Carmelite woman of the late 19th century who died of tuberculosis at the age of twenty-four. Therese talks about the death of love. All her writings are about the death of love, and they're consumed by the love of God. She really believes that's how her life is being lived out and how it's coming to an end. Now, it's interesting that the old term for that, I'm not sure what it was in French, but the old term for tuberculosis was consumption. And no doubt there was some sense of that in the European consciousness, of being consumed by this condition. Now when Therese talks about being consumed by the love of God and dying, the death of love, she is literally in those months being consumed by tuberculosis. This is also happening in historical life. Not that I'm saying that it was God who consumed her by tuberculosis, or that it was God who imprisoned John of the Cross. But these people's reflection on their experience is not just an internal reality. It's a reflection on the lived bodily experience; the historical and spiritual lives are one reality.

The most classic example of this, of course, is the crucifixion of Jesus. When Jesus had his moment of truth in the Garden of Gethsemane, asking that the cup be taken away from him, but then surrendering to the will of God, was this some charade he put on for the sake of the gospel writers, or was this a true experience, when in his historical life he had to face the fact that what he was being called to, was to walk into a total death to self, a very agonizing, painful death. The spiritual reality of that surrender was also an actual physical, historical surrender. Our spiritual and historical lives are one.

Now in following that truth, and listening to our experience, what we're going to encounter is the God of surprises. God is going to turn up, the Divine grace, the spirit, whatever word you want to use, is going to turn up in all kinds of moments and places and times and contexts where we least expect to encounter the Divine. A couple of examples of this. Jesus is the classic one, he couldn't be boxed in. Jesus as, in some sense, the love of God made flesh. He could be with the poorest of the poor, the most rejected, the most outcast, be with the prostitutes, be intimate with the prostitutes, he could also turn around and go to dinner with the Pharisees. They also said of him, this man is a drunkard and a glutton. He was also criticized because he ate with the higher classes as well as the lower classes; you can't box this guy in. He moves around, and where the grace of God in some sense is needed, or there is any level of openness, he will be there. And this is true in our lives too, the spirit will be there. In any moment where there is openness, whether we are conscious of it or not, conscious of the Spirit, or conscious of our openness, sometimes we can be becoming open without realizing it, and voom! up will come a rush of grace, a rush of the presence of God, into our consciousness. And we hadn't thought we were being spiritual at all.

I often have been asked in my ministry, my work, to invoke the Holy Spirit, to call down the Holy Spirit at the beginning of meals or weddings or academic years. And, you know, I think this is a dangerous thing. I don't think this is necessarily a good idea. People tend to do it as if this is a political thing; well, of course, you know, you invoke the Holy Spirit. Well hang on. If I invoke the spirit on your academic year, or on your wedding, or on your birthday, you better be ready for the fact that things can happen that you're not necessarily wanting to have happen. If you give over your marriage, or your life or your academic year to the Holy Spirit, you better be ready for your agenda to go out the window. This is not something to do lightly. The Holy Spirit does her own work in her own way. And we are either open or we're not. If we're not, don't invoke her. It's a sham. It's a charade. And who knows, she might just turn up and my, wouldn't we be surprised!

Now this is also very important, this idea of the God of surprises. When people work with gay and lesbian people, or when we try and support one another in the spiritual journey, I absolutely believe that sexual experiences will open us in most radical ways to the grace of God. I like to speak of the term 'the promiscuity of grace', that wherever there is a chance, grace will come in, even the slightest crack, grace will come in. And hey, there are lots of cracks. There are lots of openings in sexual experience. Could you as a director, for example, (here I speak directly to people who may be doing spiritual direction) handle it if someone came to you, having just had their first experience with S&M, for example, with sadomasochism, and they had had what they experienced as a deeply spiritual awakening. Could you handle that? Would that just be too beyond the pale, would that shatter too many of your categories? Are you prepared to believe that whatever the goods, bads, rights or wrongs, wisdom or lack of it, around what they did, can you believe that the Spirit can still come through, break through and be present in those moments? Or are you the one with the problem? If the kitchen's too hot, get out; if you can't handle this kind of promiscuity of grace, which comes from the heart of God, pursuing us in every moment, in every situation, especially in sex, then you ought not be working with gay and lesbian people. Go home, do your homework, do your own work. First, have your own awakenings, your own revelations, have your own containers shattered, then come back. And perhaps then you might be privileged enough to be ready to work with gay and lesbian people.

All that's happening here (happening in these containers of morality being shattered, or at the very least being deeply challenged) is that gay people are learning the law of the heart. There's a wonderful saying in Jeremiah, which I'll quote. Jeremiah was one of the prophets writing in Israel after the exile in Babylon. Jeremiah talks of the days when the New Covenant, the fullness, will come. And he quotes God, Yahweh, saying, 'Deep within them, I will plant my law, writing it on their hearts. There will be no further need for neighbor to try to teach neighbor, brother or sister to try and teach brother or sister. No, they will all know me, the least no less than the greatest.' One of the most beautiful quotes in Scripture, but we don't believe it. We spend our time setting up rules, regulations, telling one another how we ought to be experiencing the Divine, not trusting that now that the new covenant has come and is inviting us all into a feast of freedom and of life, that if we go deep enough, we will find this law written on our hearts.

And it is the law of freedom and love, not the law of constraints, of rigidity, of regulations. This is not to say we can't offer each other the fruit of our wisdom. But that's very different from trying to give each other boxes and ironclad rules. That is, I think, the key problem with the moral teaching of the church at the moment, not that it oughtn't be offered, but that it's offered as railway lines that stipulate that if you don't stay on the tracks, by God, you're going to have a crash or at the very least you're going to be pushed out of the train, rather than as simple lessons in wisdom that have been passed down through the centuries, which we can dialogue with, according to the law written in our own hearts. That's the only way true morality is ever passed on to anybody. Anything else is not morality at all. It's simply regulation, and being an obedient slave, being too scared to challenge in any way the rule set down by Ma or Pa or by the society around us.

Now gay and lesbian people are uniquely placed to discover this law of the heart. Why? Because if we're going to have any kind of life at all, any kind of sense of ourselves as true beings loved by God with a right to exist, we have to break the laws, we have to go outside the morality, which is so narrow that no one can live in it and be healthy. You know, in Catholic thought, for example, that you can be homosexual, but you can never, ever act on it. You can never actually be sexual. And in some of the old teaching, which came down from the Middle Ages, which is still around, you can have sex but you ought not have too much pleasure in it. There was a recent thing that came out from the Vatican saying that, actually I think it's in the new catechism, that married people do nothing wrong (interesting term) when they seek pleasure in sexual intercourse (it's very generous of them to say so), provided they do so soberly and in moderation. So I have this image of all these people around the world trying to have sober and moderate orgasms. I don't think it works. And I certainly don't think that the God of orgasms had that in mind when he/she gave us this ecstatic and glorious experience. But even within marriage, the church is still saying, here are the railway lines. Well, certainly, as a gay man, to have any sense of myself, I have to go outside of those lines, I'm forced to. And that sets me on the journey.

There are surveys (I wish I had them with me, I'm sorry that I don't) that show that gay people, and particularly gay priests who have a good sense of themselves, tend to have a higher level of moral development, according to stages like Kohlberg stages, than heterosexual people and heterosexual priests. And the reason is because we have had to walk the journey for ourselves. A couple of other little quotes: I like to throw in a beautiful one from John of the Cross, who talks about fullness of maturity in spiritual life. And he says, 'Here on the mountain, there are no laws, there are no paths, for there are no laws for the just.' Not that I'm saying we have all reached that point. I am saying that the journey to that point will move us in that direction, towards a life which has very simple laws around love, around justice, around freedom. Of course Augustine, who is much despised in a lot of modern thought, says, 'Love and do what you will, but truly love.' And that has to be our guide in our morality, to truly love.

Now, in this journey, of course, and I can't say this too strongly, there are going to be mistakes, there are going to be dead ends, people are going to go in the wrong direction. And maybe yes, tragically do some harm to ourselves in our development. But we can't not make the journey for that reason, we can't refuse to take the risks. I think of the parable of the talents in the Scripture, where the man gives one guy 10 talents, or $10, and someone else five, and someone else one, and they invest them and they make money. But the person that has one goes away and hides it in the ground. And he's the one who gets into trouble. Because hey, this thing was not given to you to hide in the ground. This was given to you to invest, to take risks with, to live your life from, not to keep safe and enclosed, which is the way we tend to look at our spiritual lives. There's a wonderful apocryphal story added on to that parable of the talents about a man who got 10 talents, took them away, invested them and lost everything. And when the master comes back, he still says, 'Well done good and faithful servant', because you took a risk, you tried it out. And that is what we have to do, taking risks but supporting one another in those risks, listening to one another and discerning together in the Spirit of God, finding balance.

Now, all of that depends upon an inner sense of love, an inner sense of truth, an inner sense of what's right, of where we're led. Now, I want to say to anyone who's directing gay and lesbian people, and to anyone who's supporting them and to us ourselves, we need to be careful of that inner sense, we need to be careful, because that inner sense has been so conditioned by our society and by our church, that what we first experienced maybe as kind of dirty or distasteful or unclean or a bit yuck can be the very thing we need to pursue. The inner sense has been really polluted in many ways by the church, by our teaching, by our parents. We all know that. So, I'm inclined to say where you find the resistances, where you find that uurh! feeling, look again, that probably is not the inner sense. The inner sense is not someone that says uurh! or someone that says, No, no, no. The inner sense is a quiet sense of wisdom and truth and clarity. It is not distaste, that's something else. And that is precisely the point where you need to fight, you need to go, you need to look.

I remember my first experiences were very painful when I first began to explore having sex with other men. And it was very hard, my conditioning was very, very deep. And I really wanted to do the truth, to do the right thing, to be in relationship with God. I had this lovely evening one time with a man. And it was delightful and simple and present. I came away, and I had the most incredible experience of wrenching, of clash, of ripping inside, because everything in me wanted to say this was bad, this was yuck, this was wrong, this was distasteful. You just had casual sex, my God, with someone you didn't know. But the truth was, I liked it. The truth was it was good. It was loving, it felt gentle, and pleasurable, and delightful and sweet. And that was the truth. And I knew that. And thanks be to God, I could not disown that, and that critiqued the yuck and the distaste and the moral conditioning. That was this ripping I felt inside, as these two parts of me kind of wrenched against each other. Well, I'll leave it to you to decide which part won.

In such experiences, of course, we need to have community. We spoke a little earlier, and we'll speak again about this. But to walk this journey is very difficult. In Latin America, communities are of the essence, you don't do this alone. We look at black families, and we look at Jewish families, and we see that these people have a basis of support, where they can be nurtured and grow and encouraged in their journey to liberation, to a sense of self, and where they can also return home to be tended and cared for and have their wounds healed. Now, we as gay people need this desperately, more so because we don't have natural families. As a director, as someone who supports gay and lesbian people, you can be vital to this sense of community. You may be the only lifeline of support that a gay person trying to live a Christian spiritual life has. And therefore you really need to be very centered, have done your own work, have dealt with your own shit, and be able to be truly present to them, truly present to the spirit within you and within them. Another one of the key things that comes from a true sense of community and a true sense of growth in the spiritual life is a sense of justice.

Now this is very clear in Latin America, it's very clear with Jewish people, it's very clear with black people. Sometimes it's not so clear with gay people. I really do believe that as a gay person grows in true spiritual fullness and wisdom, they're going to become very aware and very angry about the injustice and oppression that they suffer, that all gay people suffer, and have suffered. You will notice, for example, that when I began this talk, I invoked our gay and lesbian ancestors who have paid with their lives, in very many cases, for their love. You become very sensitive to this reality, very aware of this reality, not just in other people's lives but in our own lives. And the pain and the rage, especially with the church, can be very hard to contain, and we need to find ways of expressing it, ways of listening to one another in it.

I remember some good gay Catholic Christians being horrified by the Stop the Church action in New York City at St Patrick's. I was too at first. I remember seeing someone holding a host, a piece of communion bread, whether consecrated or not, I'm not sure. But people were horrified. As we were talking, it suddenly struck me. Where is the greatest sin: that someone could take this bread called 'This is my body' and hold it lightly and use it as a protest, or that the church could take we who are the body and violate us, abuse us, spit on us, oppress and exclude us, kill us? Where is the true violation of the body of Christ? I don't think it's in stopping mass at St Patrick's, and I don't think that's how Jesus would see it. When he said, 'This is my body', he was not primarily talking about the institution of the church. The body, which must be recognized and reverenced is here, and is here, it's in us. And when we are oppressed and violated, the body of Jesus is violated far more truly than when a host may be violated. So let us primarily reverence and adore, worship and bow before the reality of Jesus in our own bodies, and the bodies of our lesbian and gay brothers and sisters, and of all those who are oppressed. Sure let us reverence the institutions of the church when they earn it, when they truly are church, as Jesus might have meant it, although he never used the word. Let's be sensitive to them and recognize the holy, but that can only come when we truly recognize the holy within us. And let us no longer allow the body of Christ to be violated in us. Let's feel the pain and the rage of that.

Notice that a number of times in this lecture, I've spoken about maturity, the importance of maturity. When I've reflected on what maturity means for gay and lesbian people, I've often been struck by the fact that one of the main institutions of life, the main contexts in life, which heterosexual people have that tends to lead them towards maturity and adulthood, is the family, is caring for children. I'm not saying this always works (and hey, we all come from dysfunctional families), but it has a tendency to work towards maturity, simply because, day by day, year in year out, people are called to run their kids to football games, to change diapers, to help with homework, to listen to their kids when they're moaning and groaning, or when they're sick, constantly to put themselves aside and attend to the call of the children. There's also of course the wisdom and the spontaneity of children, which can shatter adult pretensions, and make us step back and realize who we are and who we are not. All the gifts that children bring.

Now, in saying that, I'm aware that surveys have shown that the average American man, for example, spends something like 12 minutes a day with his children, present with his children. So I'm not in any sense suggesting that all heterosexual couples live family as selflessly and as generously and as maturely as one would hope. But I am saying that there is this very natural, spontaneous context which most heterosexual people go into, which calls forth selflessness in time, in attention, in money, in energy and resources. And this can go on for 20 years. Now, hopefully, some lessons are being learned by people in that situation, sometimes not. But the context is there. When I've looked at gay people, I've thought, how is this for us in our spiritual lives? How do we use the extra energy, the extra time, the extra leisure and maybe the extra money? I know a lot is being said these days about our discretionary income. Well, I don't have much, I don't know about you, maybe you do, you've bought this tape. But that extra time and energy that we tend to have, whether we admit it or not, which normally people would channel into family demands, what do we do with it? What is our call in it? How can that become context for learning selflessness and maturity for us? How can this become the School of Love for us, a term the monasteries in the desert used to use?

I think that we have to look at a number of ways in which we are called to use the extra life and time and energy we have, if we're going to be mature. One of them is to live contemplatively, to truly go deeply into spiritual practice and to live very reflectively around what it means to be human, what it means to be sexual, what it means to be just, what it means to be loving, what it means to be alive, to go deeply into the spiritual life in a way that many people with families and the demands of baseball games and school picnics and things can't do. Another way is service. And here particularly we see it with AIDS, where people have been drawn into using their time and energy in deep service to one another, without realizing it. This too can be a prime way in which we can use our lives as context for growth in maturity. Another way is through art, through creativity and through study, channeling our energy and our time and our money into developing the creative gift, which expresses who we are and then can be shared with others.

Another way is through justice making, through activism, through advocacy, whether it be for us or for other oppressed groups. I might add here something that I actually forgot to include when I was talking about justice, that true justice and maturity in justice has to be opening us not just to our own oppression but to solidarity with all the oppressed. And we'll talk about that in another tape a little later on. So here are four ways: contemplative living; service; art and creativity (which is also study); and justice making. These are ways in which we, I believe, are not just able to grow to maturity but are called to grow to maturity. I'm sorry, gay energy and life and leisure are not well served by developing bigger and better and more stylish wardrobes. They are not served by developing a better interior design. They are not served by making sure we have the latest art collection, and the latest CD collection in town. They are not served by the more stylish and avant garde hairdo. I mean, these things are not necessarily bad, but they are not about growth in maturity of spiritual life. Some elements of them maybe can accompany it, God knows we all need to find ways of expressing ourselves. But when they become our focus, or our whole sense of self, something has gone awry. And I have to say, from a Christian perspective, from a spiritual perspective, this is not authentic maturity. And it certainly is not authentic liberation. It's dancing around the golden calf. We'll talk about that in the third tape, what that means.

Now, of course, one of our problems in all of this is the lack of models. To learn to live a mature and integrated spiritual gay life, we need models, we need mentors, and there are so few of them. And many of the few we have have died from AIDS, or are dying of AIDS, or are so engrossed in caring for people with AIDS, they're not available for others. There is a desperate need for mature models of Christian, and generally spiritual, gay life. And there is a call to us, I believe, to become those models. I would like to think that people who are directors could, in some sense, be something of that kind of a model. There's a challenge.

In all of this about growth and maturity, it's important to mention briefly the place of psychotherapy and the place of spiritual direction. We, as gay people have come through so much emotional and psychological pain and shit. Psychotherapy, good psychotherapy, good counseling, is a good idea for everyone in our crazy culture. But for us, it's probably something of a necessity in many cases, in most cases, if we're going to grow to true maturity. At the same time, I would like to differentiate between psychotherapy and spiritual direction or spiritual guidance or spiritual practice. They're not discontinuous, and they're not totally separate, but nor are they totally one and the same thing. I do believe that a lot of psychotherapy is a prerequisite, a precursor for deep spiritual living. But I also believe that spiritual life and particularly contemplative life takes us where psychotherapy could never go. It takes us into a depth of centeredness, into a depth of selflessness. It shatters our containers and it rebuilds us in a way that psychotherapy cannot do. And it calls us to a death of self, which psychotherapy is not about, but all true spiritual living is about. And here, I don't mean some pathological, hysterical death of self, I mean a deep, profound surrender of the self. As I say, [psychotherapy] may well be a necessary precursor to a deep spiritual life, or an accompaniment; but spiritual life and I think spiritual guidance are slightly different and need their own focus and their own time. Of course, it's important to discern when and where and how psychotherapy is needed, spiritual direction is needed.

This also brings up the issue of talking about direction, spiritual guidance, the readiness of the director, the readiness of the guide. This person must be someone who has really done their work or is profoundly doing their work, someone who really has dealt with a lot of their inner demons, and a lot of their inner containers. The person who I go to for spiritual guidance uses the default zone. Apparently, in dealing with computers, which I don't deal with, you do defaults to set up margins. And he's suggesting that in spiritual life, those defaults are gradually expanded and eventually blown away. Well, a person who's going to give direction to gay people has to have very few defaults, very few limitations, very few margins, and be prepared to let go of the ones they do have. Part of the reason for this is that I really believe a gay person coming to someone for spiritual guidance is a gift to that spiritual director. And they are going to take your categories, your ideas, your concepts, your understandings of God, of spirit, of body, and stand them on their head, turn them upside down, turn them inside out. And if you can't handle that, then don't do the work. If you're not prepared to be shattered yourself (I suppose I speak especially to heterosexual directors and heterosexual guides), if you're not prepared to have those categories shattered, don't do the work.

You also need to be very careful of softly giving judgments to a gay person. Sometimes if our categories are being shattered, we want someone to tell us that the old story, the old rule was the truth. Like that night when I had that clash and felt, this is good. No, this can't be good. I've been told this is terrible. And I've taken it in. If I'd had a spiritual guide who in the subtlest way suggested that the voice of the old rule was the true voice, and not this voice, which told me that this sexual experience was good, I may well have gone with that judgment, that restriction, that old morality.

You're very sensitive and vulnerable when you're going through this process of allowing the containers to be shattered, and judgments are picked up very quickly. So as a director, you have to step back and let go of your judgments very purely. Don't be frightened to admit you can't do the work, you can't work with the gay or lesbian person. Okay, in all of this you also need to be a very good waiter, someone who can wait, then someone who can affirm because the journey is not quick, it's not easy. You need to be able to wait with the person on the guidance of the Holy Spirit.

Just a couple of very crucial points to close this talk, that in a sense go to the foundation of spiritual life, and that I believe are essential in understanding the gay journey. Firstly (I'll say this very briefly, we'll develop it in the next talk), the absolute goodness and centrality of the incarnation of Christ, the goodness and centrality of sexuality, that when God becomes human, when God becomes flesh, which is a central mystery of the Christian religion, whether we understand it as literally true or whether we understand it as a profound myth that informs our lives, this is absolutely crucial to the spiritual journey. God is human: bodily, sexually, viscerally, with guts, with energy, with pain, with drives and urges and juices (in Dame Edna Everage's terms), juices, with the fullness of what it means to be human. And all of that, every part of that, especially perhaps the parts that we find hardest to own, our sexuality, our anus, our guts, our shit, all of this becomes saturated, impregnated, filled with the Divine. So that now there is nothing human that can separate us from the presence of God, because all that is Divine has come fully into all that is human. St Paul says, 'but without sin.' Okay, but also entering into the drives, the needs, the compulsions, the pains, the pathologies, the neuroses, that give rise to sin. All of those are not sin and in some sense, all of those God enters into too. All that is fully human is now impregnated with the Divine. So every human experience, every human moment, every human touch, every activity of the human can now become a vehicle of the Divine, a channel for the Divine, a way of entering into the Divine, and most especially the sexual, where we experience the juice of life itself, the creative urge itself, the urge to communion itself. That, most of all, is going to be impregnated with the Divine, saturated with the Divine. Again, we'll go into this a little more in the second talk.

Secondly, in Christian spirituality, there are two ways, and this will become clear in the second tape, and in the third tape. The first is the *kataphatic* way, the affirmative way, the *Via Positiva*. And what this is, well, look at it this way: think of every word you've ever heard about God, every scripture passage you've ever heard, every ritual you've ever attended, or seen performed, or heard of, every piece of theology, every single prayer, every statue or image you've ever seen. Now, along with that, think of every creature that exists, every sunset, every plant, every animal, every star, every thought, every concept, every feeling, every 'thing' that our mind can in any way comprehend or grasp, in any way that our mind can use. Anything that is accessible directly to the senses and the mind is the *kataphatic* way, it's the affirmative way. All of those things lead us to God, or can lead us to God. All that can be thought, imagined, tasted, touched, felt, seen, heard, everything, is the *kataphatic* or the affirmative way.

The *apophatic* way is everything else. The *apophatic* way is the absolute silence, the absolute darkness, the absence of images, the absence of thought, of concept, of feeling, of visions, of statues, the absence of creatures, the absolute stillness and silence beyond thought, beyond word, beyond image, the absolute mystery, that which is unsayable, unspeakable, unable to be conceptualized in any form, the Divine darkness, the absolute unknowing. This is the *apophatic*, the dark, the negative way, the *Via Negativa*.

And this is in us too, this is the absolute mystery, which we encounter at the depths of our being, underneath all that we can conceptualize, or can contain in our minds. And whatever leads us into that darkness and that silence is the *apophatic* way, the way of darkness and negation. God is not that, not that, not that. God is not even God! God is silence. But even silence is not God. God is beyond even silence. Now to work with gay and lesbian people, or to follow this journey as a gay or lesbian person, I think you need to do your homework around these two ways, the *kataphatic* way and the *apophatic* way, because I believe they are very, very powerfully present in the lives of all gay and lesbian people. Both ways are very richly present.

And finally, our companion, our guide, our touchstone, our joyous lover on the journey has to be a sense of celebration, a sense of hope, a sense of joy. Someone said that joy is the infallible sign of the presence of God. And by joy, I don't just mean levity or lightness or happiness as our culture tends to define it. Someone once said the most unfortunate term ever coined is 'the pursuit of happiness', that happiness is something we have to in some sense chase. Joy, rather, wells up from the deepest part of us. It's a feeling of a sense of well-being, a sense of possibility, a sense of goodness, a sense of hope that somehow there is life in all of this, even if it be the tiniest flicker at the very bottom of the well. Even if it be the tiniest seed, which almost looks dead. There is always the possibility of new life coming from that. And that is joy.

Now as gay and lesbian people, we need to really be with that joy, be open to that joy, believe in that joy, walk with that joy, because this journey is a very difficult and demanding one. There are few guides, there are few supports, especially in contemplative living and in gay living where the church tends to oppose our gayness, and gay people often tend to oppose our contemplativeness and especially our Christianity. We have to have a deep sense of joy and believe in joy. So my wish for us, as we close this first talk, is that joy may be our accompaniment and our guide, our touchstone, our lover, as we journey on. And as St Francis said at the end of his life as he lay dying, 'brothers and sisters, let us begin'.

Study Guide

The truth of our experience offers a general introduction to the course, and includes some notes and suggestions for spiritual directors. Areas considered include:

Our spiritual journey as one of liberation, requiring a true theology of liberation which calls us:

- To see our actual situation
- To believe that things could be different, as we analyse the causes of oppression and consider strategies for change and transformation
- To reclaim and re-imagine Scripture and Tradition as our story
- To form communities of resistance and support.

The role of the Spiritual Director or Spiritual Companion:

- Education and formation, including the central role of personal experience
- Patience, quiet and faithful accompaniment, deep listening
- Being ready to be challenged, stretched, surprised and transformed
- Trusting in God's initiative as this emerges in real life and in patterns and lessons that only take form over a lifetime.

The central importance of owning the deep truths of our own experience—our 'spiritual' and 'historical' lives are not separate. We live one life.

The God of Surprises; the 'promiscuity of grace'; the freedom of the Holy Spirit.

Moral decision making and discerning the 'law written on the heart'.

The 'School of Love' for gay and lesbian people.

The need for true elders, mentors, guides, models.

The 'Affirmative' (or Cataphatic) Way, and the 'Negative' (or *Apophatic*) Way, of spiritual and mystical growth.

The core importance of Celebration and Hope.

Regarding the complex issues around terms like 'gay', 'lesbian', 'queer' and 'LGBTIQ+', please see the extended *Note on Language* in the General Introduction. The series was recorded in 1994, and generally follows the accepted conventions of the time.

Questions for discussion and reflection

1. What story or passage from Scripture has been most helpful and enriching for you as an LGBTIQ+ person?

2. What is the most difficult challenge we face in reclaiming Scripture and Tradition for LGBTIQ+ people? How could we work creatively with this?

3. Liberation? Consider the actual situation we face as LGBTIQ+ Christians, as you see it today. What does 'Liberation' mean to you? How committed are you (as an individual or as a group) to this journey of Liberation? What would it be like, feel like, look like?

4. Consider the reality of what we sometimes call the 'queer community', or the 'gay community', or the 'LGBTIQ+ community'? What kind of community do LGBTIQ+ Christians truly need? Be daring in your vision! How could you help to nurture such community?

5. Who have been your spiritual guides, mentors, and models? Who inspired and/or supported you during your 'coming out'? Who do you look to for guidance and inspiration as you mature in life as an LGBTIQ+ person of faith? Could you imagine becoming such a mentor, guide or model for others?

6. 'Coming Out'—both within yourself and externally in family, church, society and world'—where you are personally on this journey? How do you understand God's call in this area? What is helping you, or hindering you in responding fully and freely to this call?

7. 'The God of Surprises' and the 'Promiscuity of Grace'. What do these terms mean to you? How have you experienced this in your own life, or how have you seen this emerging in the lives of others? How do you handle giving up control in these deeper areas of your life?

8. Has your own 'inner sense' conflicted with 'Religious Authority'? How have you tended to handle and/or resolve this conflict? How do you feel the Holy Spirit is calling you to deal with this conflict—both today, and over your lifetime?

9. The 'School of Love' is that which teaches us daily self-giving. What is this school of love for you in your personal life, and in your communal life? Do you think that living authentically as an LGBTIQ+ person of faith can become a school of love for you?

10. Celebration. What is the difference between true celebration and 'partying'? In your own life, what draws you into a spirit of deep celebration? Are there ways in which you block this? How can you and your community bring more 'rituals of joy' into your life?

2

Re-visioning Sex and Sexuality

It's possible that whilst sleeping, the hand that sowed the seeds of stars started the ancient music going again, like a note from a great harp, and the frail wave comes to our lips as one or two honest words.

Machado

The poem by Machado speaks of 'one or two honest words'. Whenever we deal with sexuality, especially in relation to spirituality, we need to be very aware that we're dealing with a great and very profound mystery. And the most we can hope is that out of our sense of the mystery, and out of our own experience, we can say one or two honest words. But those are words that are very, very needed in our time and in our culture.

I'd like to stress, too, the exploratory nature of all that I'll say in this talk. In some ways, I'm trying new categories, trying new ways of looking at sexuality, at ways we might think, new ways of wondering. Nothing that I'm saying is prescriptive or proscriptive. All I'm saying is exploratory. And perhaps some of it may speak to your heart and to your own exploration, and your own spiritual journey; that would be my hope. It's important that we be aware of the need that causes us to speak, that not just ourselves as gay and lesbian people, but the whole of our culture is very split apart in terms of spirituality and sexuality—not just divided, but in conflict with one another. Hence, our incredible condemnation of the sexual on the one hand, and our absolutely obsessive fascination with it on the other; these, the two sides of the one coin of repression.

So there is this crying need, I think, in all people, not just in gay and lesbian people, to find new ways of thinking about sexuality, keeping in mind always that it is fundamentally a mystery, which is alive in our bodies but mysterious nonetheless. Needless to say, we can't do any of this unless we tell the truth of our experience, and actually reflect on it. A recent famous theologian was writing that one of the problems in Western culture is that we've been quick to talk about the need for spirit or mind to rule the body, and to rule its imperious passions. And we've been less ready to talk about the gifts that body gives to spirit. And that's something of what I want to do in this talk. Look at the truth of our bodies and the gifts they give us.

I was noticing that this can even be very hard for modern day spiritual teachers. I recently looked at a new book called *The Ground We Share* by two masters, a Christian and a Buddhist, who are well-renowned in this country and internationally. Of the whole book, maybe ten pages even referred to sexuality. Most of those were on sexual misconduct of gurus, on issues of molestation of children, on celibate sexuality; there was virtually no reference, except maybe on one or two pages, to sexuality at all. And this is 1994. And these are a Buddhist and a Christian teacher who are both well-respected in New Age circles as well as traditional ones.

What are we doing? Where do we expect our spirituality to come from if we keep editing out the sexual? Part of the problem (why this is so difficult, especially in the Christian tradition as we find it today) is there's a tremendous climate of fear in the church, with the current regime of John Paul the second. There's also a great sense of fear in society, as the religious right moves forward and tries to overthrow the little bit of sexual freedom that we have, the sexual exploration we're engaging in. The second reason why it's difficult is that we have 2000 years of not reflecting on our sexual experience, of pushing it aside, of repressing it or, at best, ignoring it. So it's very hard to now come and talk about it. Thirdly, we have a tendency, both in our church and in our culture, to speak as if we know, as if we have the truth, and we will communicate it to you. Now sexuality is so complex and profound that no one has the full truth. And again, it's very hard for our church and our society to accept the exploratory nature of what we say about sex. Fourthly, of course, we all carry individually the legacy of shame, the shame of our conditioning, the shame our culture has taught us. And this also makes it difficult to speak.

All of our theology and our spirituality has been done in this climate. John McNeil, a Jesuit priest who was expelled from the Jesuits for his work with gay and lesbian people, says that all our wells, all our traditional wells of wisdom are polluted by homophobia. I'm sure Carter Heywood would add erotophobia. And so, when we try to drink from these wells, it's very hard to get a pure taste of what they're saying to us. The current situation in the church makes it very risky to do this work that I'm doing today. And therefore the conversations that need to happen are not happening. People are tending to cover their backs and be careful in what they say. Desperate conversations that people are hungry for, discussions, not dogmas or doctrines, but just discussions, are not taking place. Please God, this class, this lecture can be one of those conversations, one of those discussions. I would like you to take it as such. Secondly, even the most daring amongst our theologians tend only to focus on long-term monogamous relationships when they talk about sexuality. And the problem is that not all gay and lesbian people by any means live in long-term monogamous relationships. So a lot of our sexual experience is edited out, edited away.

I remember listening recently to Bishop Spong in Melbourne, in Australia where I live, one of the most daring and courageous modern churchmen in the US. And when it came to talking about sex, he was quite eloquent. But towards the end, he stressed, I'm only talking about long-term monogamous relationships, anything outside of that, in terms of sexuality, is destructive. Now, I think Spong has *written* somewhat differently. But this was what he said, I heard him. This sense of covering our backs, that we not be caught saying things we can be taken to task for.

A second point that I would like to make in relation to this is that this goes against the wisdom that we have been given in our modern church. For example, the Second Vatican Council, one of the most seminal moments in the history of the Catholic church, and by implication, the universal church, said in one of its most important documents, *The Church in the Modern World*, that what we have to learn to do is to listen to the wisdom of the Holy Spirit speaking in other cultures and other religions. This was a very important move away from the idea that we had the fullness of the truth, and only we had the truth, to recognize [that] the spirit is alive in everyone. Now, this was a beautiful thing to say. And it's revolutionized a lot of our theology, but we don't do it when it comes to sexuality. We don't look at the sexual wisdom, the sexual traditions and customs, the religious practices that involve sexuality, in other times and cultures and tribes, and listen for the Holy Spirit there. We edit out, again, the sexual.

Underlying all of this, I believe, is the hidden and sometimes not-so-hidden understanding that sex is not good. That in some way it needs to be justified. Now, for most of Christian history, this was done by invoking procreation: that sex (and often it was said quite straightforwardly) was an evil and it was justified by procreation. Now, we've gone beyond most of this, but a lot of modern theologians and moral theologians are talking as if sex is justified in a long-term monogamous relationship, that this is what justifies sex. Personally, I can't see that this is such a great improvement. We're still saying sex needs to be justified, firstly by procreation, now by long-term monogamous relationships. Now something that needs to be justified is not inherently good. We read in Genesis (it's fundamental stuff) that all that God created, 'behold, it was very good.' Six times, it was good, it was good, it was good, it was good, it was very good, all of it. Surely sex and sexuality, the very driving force of the universe, the juice for communion with other people and with God, has to come into that goodness, has to also be an essential part of that goodness, has to share in that goodness. So therefore sex in itself does not need to be justified. It is already good.

Sure, that's not to say that any good, (food, sleep, drink, community, any good) can't be polluted, or in some way distorted or used in destructive ways. Of course it can. But therefore the criteria we need to look at are: when might sex become not so good, not so helpful, not so growth producing? When might it become a little destructive?—rather than, when might sex be good, when might sex be justified?, which is the way we are still thinking when we invoke justifications in terms of long-term monogamous relationships. This harks back to one of the ancient heresies in the church, the question of whether or not human nature is fundamentally good, or fundamentally evil. Now, the idea that human nature is fundamentally evil was absolutely condemned in the early centuries of the church. Human nature is fundamentally good. Now, it seems to me that if human nature is fundamentally good, sexuality and sex and sexual relating are good in themselves as integral to human nature.

So given all that (and this is the climate in which we make our explorations in this tape, a climate in which the church is still struggling to even begin to say sex is good), we move forward with great gusto and courage to suggest some far more radical ideas than just that sex is good. So please come along for the ride.

Firstly, many today, not so much in the church, but also partly in the church, talk about the integration of sexuality and spirituality, and this is, of course, a great need. There is some attempt to say even, that sexuality and spirituality are the same, that they are the one energy. Recently I heard even a Catholic contemplative monk, who is involved in guidance for younger monks in an order in Berkeley, actually say that they are the same energy.

Now, I think there's something in us that recognizes that this is deeply true. And it's a very, very appealing concept that sexuality and spirituality are in fact the one energy. And yet, it also seems to me as a gay man that when I look at a lot of what goes on in sex, say in San Francisco, in pornography, in a lot of the different writings that you read, and practices that probably many of us have engaged in, some of that makes me feel it's not quite so simple. That yes, they are the one energy, and it's not quite that simple. There's something in me that says, when I see some of what goes on in sexual practices, this is not just all these people being holy, or all these people doing spiritual practice. For some of them, I think it probably is, but for some of them equally I don't feel that this is the simple truth of all that is going on here. So what can we say? What could we possibly say about sexuality and spirituality?

I'd like to offer you my exploration, one concept that I would like to suggest. It's tentative, and in some ways it's bold, but I hope it may be helpful as a way of wondering about sex and spirituality. The heart of it is to say yes, they are the same energy. They are the same pure water of the uncreated life of God coming to us very directly in sexuality and in spirituality; it is ultimately the one water. And to back up this fairly daring statement, I'd like to read for you a couple of quotes from a very, very ancient text in Christian scripture called the Song of Songs, which may be familiar to some of you. For many years, well for 2500 years, there has been an argument going on amongst scripture scholars and theologians as to whether or not this is about sexual love, or whether this is an allegory of divine love and human love, of the union between Christ and the church, the union of God and His people. So just listen to it as a sexual poem; these are just a few excerpts. Remember this is 2500 years old.

> Oh, for your kiss, for your love, more enticing than wine, for your scent, and sweet name. For all this, they love you. So take me away to your room, like a king to his rooms. We'll rejoice there with wine. No wonder they love you. I sleep but my heart stirs and dreams. My lover's voice here at the door. Open my love, my

sister, my dove, my perfect one, for my hair is soaked with the night. Should I get up, get dressed and dirty my feet? My love thrusts his hand at the latch. When my heart leaps up for him, I rise to open for my love, my hands tripping perfume on the lock. Oh, of all pleasure, how sweet is the taste of love. Your breasts will be tender as clusters of grapes. Your breath will be sweet as the fragrance of quince and your mouth will awaken all sleeping desire, like wine that entices the lips of new lovers. Stamp me in your heart. Upon your limbs sear my emblem deep into your skin. For love is strong as death, harsh as the grave. Its tongues are flames, a fierce and holy flame.

Now, for 2000 years and including today, they are still arguing, is this just a sexual poem, or is this an allegory of the union of the soul with God? In other words, these two realities are so close that after all this time, we still cannot decide whether this is primarily this, or primarily this. The realities are so much the same. I don't know about you, but what I hear is something very erotic, and very, very spiritual, and that's as it should be. This same text, the Song of Songs, is probably one of the most, if not the most, fundamental texts in Christian mysticism. So many of our mystics and our spiritual writers draw from the Song of Songs when they try to express or image what it means to be united with the divine; it is from this erotic poem that they primarily draw their imagery and their sources, and that they return to. This too is saying something very powerful about the union of sexuality and spirituality as the one energy. So I would like to offer you a very simple diagram, a very simple image, of how I understand the sexual and the spiritual and their relationship to one another. Because as I said, although they are the one pure water, in some sense, it's not that simple.
So we'll look at this rather awful diagram that I have drawn up to get some models, some image, of what I'm saying. This is actually supposed to be a river, amazingly enough, which runs in two courses.

The river comes from a deep source underground, that's why I haven't finished this, it goes underground, into a hiddenness. As it rises from the ground with great power and richness, it travels along in one course for a while, but then it splits into two courses, which are roughly parallel, which then spread out into all kinds of other streamlets and rivulets on both sides. Now, if we take this one to be the sexual, and this one to be the spiritual, what I'm suggesting is that they fundamentally both come from the one source, and they are the same water flowing from the hidden source deep underground, right out into all the small rivulets, all the other streamlets, as they spread out into the ground, giving life and bringing fruit. Now, I'm suggesting that the nature of the water is that it wants to draw us upstream. We taste it and it wants to draw us back; we get that sense, like a salmon, that we're called to swim upstream towards the source there, in fact, to die, which may be something of the deep connection between sexuality and spirituality and death. As these two courses come closer together, they run more deeply and more richly, and they begin to overlap, streams begin to move from one to the other. And even up here, there are occasionally streams that move closer and closer to each other. And in this, I'm suggesting that in deep spiritual experience, as well as in deep sexual experience, firstly, we taste the water of life, the water of God, at increasingly deep levels, and it draws us closer to the other side as well.

Deep sexual experience tends to draw us towards the spiritual, deep spiritual experience tends to draw us towards the sexual. And gradually as we go deeper and deeper into both, the water becomes one, and there is no way of differentiating between the sexual and the spiritual. In fact at this point, in some ways, both courses go underground. We'll talk about that a little later in the lecture. Out here, where the water is spreading out and giving life, it can also move into marshes and bogs and dead ends, so that people can be engaging in all kinds of sexual practices, which may or may not be drawing them back down towards the source, but in which they are still tasting, in fact, the water. Similarly, in spirituality, people can be engaging in all kinds of spiritual practices, which do not draw them back to the source, maybe getting them bogged down in things like fundamentalism or dogmatism, but they are still in some sense tasting a little of the water and feeling something of its longing.

So I am saying that in all sexual experience, no matter how simple and in some ways trivial it may seem, there is a real taste of the water of the divine, and that is essential to the delight and the lure, the enticement we feel when we have or seek any kind of sexual experience. I'm also saying that is the enticement and the allure in any kind of spiritual experience, the same allure, and its nature is to draw us deeper, to draw us upstream, again, like the salmon towards the source. Now we'll develop this image a little later on. But the key thing I'm suggesting is they are the same energy in two sources, two courses, two channels.

I'd like to reminisce with you for a moment about what your first sexual experience was like. About what that first moment of orgasm was like the first time you tasted it. I think there was probably a sense of, This is it! Wow! As if somehow you've touched the most delightful thing you've ever encountered, or ever could encounter, as if everything you ever wanted or dreamt was happening in that simple one moment, this great awakening, which was at the same time, this simple pure moment of intense pleasure. I think universally there is this feeling of, This is it! Now, if we could reminisce also for a moment about your first true spiritual experience, the first moment you truly felt the movement of the spirit of the Divine within, I think there's the same sense of, This is it! I've tasted it, it's come alive. This is it. This is what they're talking about, the spiritual truth present in us, these same dynamics, the sense of having found the essence, that which everyone is seeking, in however small a form. Again it's the same essence, it's the same water that we're tasting.

This pure and wonderful awakening reminds me of a few different teachings I'd like to share with you. It's a common teaching in

Tibetan Buddhism, and amongst a lot of yoga practitioners, that at the moment of orgasm, whether consciously or unconsciously, everyone attains pure mind, we attain the purity of the essence of being, whether consciously or unconsciously. I think too, for example, of something Heidegger said, which is that the mystery, the essential trait of the mystery, is that which shows itself and at the same time withdraws. And in those first sexual and spiritual experiences, we have the same sense; here is the mystery, I found it, and at the same moment, it's gone. It withdraws. This is the nature of sexual delight. It's also the nature of the mystery of God. I think too of one of our modern spiritual writers, John S Dunne, who says that underneath all of our other desires, there is the one pure desire, our heart's desire, which is the desire for God. And he quotes TE Lawrence, Lawrence of Arabia, who once had an old man who came out of the desert from nowhere and said to him, 'The love is from God, and of God, and towards God,' and then went away again. And Lawrence remembered that all of his life. And John S Dunne uses that as a symbol to say that all of our longing, all of our desire, which is awakened by these first experiences, is in fact the desire for God, the desire for the true pure water.

Starhawk says that sex is the manifestation of the driving force energy of the universe, that sexuality is an expression of the moving force that underlies everything and gives it life. And something DH Lawrence says, which I love, is that the magnificent here and now of life in the flesh is ours and ours alone, and ours only for a time; we ought to dance with rapture, spiritual ecstasy, that we should be alive and in the flesh and part of the living incarnate cosmos. Again, the sexual and the spiritual, united in one ecstasy of rapture. Susan Griffin says that the nature of all our wanting, all our desire is that it leads us to the sacred. Julian of Norwich speaks of living in love's longing. And Julian was a great spiritual mystic. Every lover knows what she means. Irenaeus speaks of the glory of God as the human fully alive; fully alive surely involves the sexual. Jesus speaks of his gift as being to bring us life in its fullness. Truly, this also involves the fullness of sexual being; life, spirit, God, union, sex are all the one same reality, the same union, the same driving force, the same water that we seek to taste ever more deeply. It seems to me that the contemplative (and we're speaking in this tape about the erotic contemplative) is a person who instinctively knows this, that there is one source, there is one energy, there is one desire, and the contemplative, most of all, is one who is prepared to sell everything and seek the pearl of great price, as the Gospel says, who is prepared to make this longing and this search, this movement upstream to the source, the center of his or her life. And rather than seeing sex as a distraction from this journey, from this search, we need to see it as one of the prime sources in which we taste the water, and in which we are drawn ever more deeply into the water. Sex is not a distraction from the spiritual; as the Song of Song says, it is a flash of fire, a flame of Yahweh himself that we experience in erotic love, in erotic lovemaking.

So, what is happening when we have sex, particularly sex at a deep level? It's communion. It's merging. It's a oneness with our partner, and with the universe. It's a self-transcendence. Even in simple sexual pleasure, you can watch someone's face and see the ego boundaries beginning to dissolve, see the hard sense of self softening as they enter into their pleasure. At its highest form, of course, it's a total ecstatic self-transcendence. It's also a deep acceptance of ourselves, of our vulnerability, and acceptance of the other in vulnerability. It's also, I think, primarily a sense of presence. The now is very intense and very real. You can't be fully present in sexuality unless all of your mind, your heart, your body is focused on what is happening in the body, in the presence of sex. Fantasies, though they can have their use, tend to split us off from that. And we need to return more and more to just the simple presence of pure sex.

There was always, it seems to me, a taste of the inarticulable. No matter what we say about sex, we know we haven't got it. We haven't said what needs to be said. We haven't summed it up. There's something that eludes us in anything we say about sex, anything we think about sex. That's probably why we say so much, because we can't get it. It's mystery. It's a taste of the mystery. A couple of lines from this modern theologian I was mentioning, Mary Pellauer, when she speaks of the skin of the lover, of the beloved, as an icon of the universe, a window into the mystery of the universe. Myself, I remember an intense experience of lovemaking when it suddenly flooded through me that I didn't know who it was I was making love to, not just in the sense that I may not have known this person's name, but rather that I was making love to someone at a profound level, and it wasn't simply this person here. I think many of us have had that experience, that we're in some way in communion with the divine mystery in sex, in lovemaking.

How can we possibly doubt the holiness of sex, the sacredness of sex, the spirituality of sex, when these terms of merging, of soft transcendence, of oneness, of communion, of vulnerability, of absolute presence, of inarticulable mystery, are the very terms we use about spiritual experience, they're the very categories we go to to talk about spiritual experience. Sexuality also brings us into them. So we taste something of God, and it is through our bodies and it is through our pleasure, this deeply spiritual experience. We are one bodily and spiritual reality.

Now compare this with the incredible body-negativity that we have been handed by our church and by our culture, the fear of pleasure. One of the things that came from the Middle Ages was the idea that it was okay, for example, for men to have erections. The problem was enjoying them, to enter into the pleasure. That was the issue, enjoying the pleasure—that was where the sin was found, this fear of pleasure, when in fact it's one of the greatest gifts of God. John Giles Milhaven, who's again a modern theologian, says this, that real pleasures are dangerous because they are real. We know we're, in a sense, tasting the truth. And they give the person who feels those pleasures a touchstone of reality. They are most dangerous because they can peel off from the person's sensibility, the crust formed by the vanity, the bustle, the irony and the tedium of the world. They peel off the crust. Such pleasures make the person feel that he is coming home, she is coming home, recovering themselves, who they truly are. In other words, if one is open to these pleasures, one experiences one's recovery of self, true self.

Now that quote actually comes from a section where he is quoting CS Lewis, and his *Screwtape Letters*. Screwtape, who is the devil, an image of the devil, is complaining that people should not be allowed to experience these sorts of pleasures, because they enter into the true self, and they open the person to God. So Screwtape wants to stop this kind of pleasure. One wonders what the church has been doing for so long, playing Screwtape's game, stopping people from experiencing the fullness of pleasure, which leads us into ourselves and into God. This, I think is something that all true lovers know, that deep pleasure takes us deeply into who we are and opens us to the other and to self-transcendence. It's also something all true saints know, that deep pleasure is at the heart of spiritual experience. This is why they break out into such ecstatic language as we'll see in a little while, because they know the depth of pleasure.

There's something very extravagant about the sensuousness of God. Have you ever walked along a beach at sunset and just thought, this is completely over the top, this riot of sensuality with sound and taste and smell and vision, this gorgeous lovemaking with the sky and the earth and the ocean. This is what God gives us, drawing us into a sensual experience of the divine in creation, in all things. Truly I want to say that our God is a sensuous and loving God. And that deep pleasure, real pleasure, true pleasure, is her epiphany, is her embrace, and is her enticement. So unless we open our souls and ourselves to true pleasure, we can never really advance, never really deepen our spiritual lives. Indeed, why would we go on this journey at all, if it was not for the pleasure beyond pleasure. None of this denies that we can get stuck and dissipate our energies in mindless rather than mindful pleasure seeking. But to deny the richness of this reality for the sake of some of the risks is to deny life itself.

So the person who's newly awakened in sexuality and spirituality sets about seeking more of this water, tasting more deeply. Religious activities, once routine, become filled with joy and meaning and the presence of God. Sexual experiences, our sleeping bodies come alive with a sense of juiciness and delight. And we experience our longing, our longing to go deeper. This is really what this awakening is for, to seduce us, to entice us deeper and deeper into the water. As we go deeper, following our diagram, as I was saying, we find that our sexual experiences and our spiritual experiences start to overlap and become one. And our longing leads us into this union of these two. At times, you don't know whether you're longing for God or longing for the beloved, to make love with you in the afternoon. It becomes the one thing and the image of God as the divine lover, which is so universal in spiritual traditions. What are we talking about? We're talking about the one longing, the one desire. I'd like to read a few quotes from people who make love, and then a few quotes from people who have had deep spiritual experiences and you can listen to the crossovers.

> At the moment of orgasm itself, I melt into existence and it melts into me. I am most fully embodied in this explosion of nerves, and also broken open into the cosmos. I am rent open, I am cleaved and joined not only to my partner, but to everything, everything as my beloved, or vice versa, has also become me. The puny walls of my tiny separate personhood drop so that I, you, he, she, we, they, are one or they build up so thoroughly that all of me is one. And if I let myself love, let myself touch, enter my own pleasure and longing, enter the body of another, the darkness, let the dark parts of my body speak, as I enter into the body's language, tongue into mouth, a part of me that I believed was real begins to die. I

descend into matter. I know I am at the heart of myself, and I cry out in ecstasy. For in love, we surrender our uniqueness and become world.

And from a mystic—Beatrice of Nazareth, from the 16th century:

> From the depths of God's wisdom, he shall teach you what he is, and what wonderful sweetness the one lover lives in the other and so permeates the other that they do not know themselves from each other. But they possess each other in mutual delight, mouth in mouth, heart in heart, body in body, soul in soul. While a single divine nature flows through them both, and they both become one through each other, yet remaining all themselves.

St Teresa of Avila has that famous passage where she speaks of an angel standing next to her and driving a fiery dart deep into her heart, and then drawing it out.

> When he drew it out, I thought he was drawing out my entrails, and with it, he left me completely afire with great love for God. The pain was so sharp that it made me utter several moans, and so excessive was the sweetness caused by this intense pain that one can never wish to lose it. Nor will one's soul be content with anything less than God. It is not bodily pain but spiritual, though the body has a share in it, indeed a great share.

Or John of the Cross who says,

> Upon my flowery breast, kept wholly for himself alone, there he stayed sleeping and I caressed him, and the fanning of the cedars made a breeze. The wind blew from the turret as I parted his locks, and his gentle hand wounded my neck, and caused all my

> senses to be suspended. I remained lost in oblivion, my face I
> reclined on my beloved. And I abandoned myself, leaving my
> cares forgotten amongst the lilies.

Now, who is speaking of lovemaking and who is speaking of divine union? You see how, as the mystics come closer to the sexual, to come deeper in the water, they begin to use sexual language. As people having deep sex come closer to the deepest water, they begin to use mystical language, the two begin to become one. One hardly knows where one begins and the other ends.

Now, I'm not necessarily totally equating all deep lovemaking with the heights of mystical experience experienced by the saints. But there is definitely the same water, the same energy at work. We'll say a little more about this later on. So also, as I was indicating in the diagram, as the two channels, the two energies, the two ways of experiencing the water, come closer together, they also in some sense, go underground.

Now, in the spiritual life, this is referred to as the dark night of the soul. It's a term that's probably been used and abused a little much these days. In contemplative literature, it really refers to a deep and very searing death of the self, a total remaking of the whole person, which shakes up all the understandings of themselves or God or life. It also is often used in terms of ordinary emotional pain. But technically, it really is a very specific moment in spiritual life, which not everyone comes to. It's a very deep level of prayer, even though it feels like the whole personality is falling apart.

Now, I'd also like to suggest that as this water of sexuality comes deeper and flows in with this same stream, we begin to experience possibly a kind of a dark night of sex. This is something I've never heard anyone talk about. But what I have heard people talk about (and even people who have a lot of sex and a lot of deep sex) is a kind of a death, a dying, an emptying out of sex and of what it means for them, that there is an unease, a sense of this is not enough, there needs to be more here. And often they're looking for a deeper spiritual life, a more contemplative way of being present, as if what gave them the taste before now is a little empty; it's still there, but it's not doing what it was doing before. And I think this (if used well and wisely) can lead us into a kind of dark night of sexuality where sex too becomes emptied out, and allows us to become emptied out, and enter into a deeper life of the spirit. This was partly why I was not equating totally deep sexual experience with deep spiritual experience, because the mystics have been through this dark night. And I think that in going through the dark night fully, we also have to go through it sexually. Some of our sexual delights and our sexual joy and some of our sexual experiences have to fall apart too. But I think this can happen in quite ordinary ways.

Someone commented once that you can obviously tell the church's sexual teaching was written by celibates, because anyone who's in a long-term monogamous relationship, or has a lot of sex, knows that sooner or later the problem is maintaining desire, not controlling it, maintaining the ardour, not suppressing it. There is a kind of limitation to some of the sexual drive and some of the sexual desire we have, if it's given its full freedom. Sooner or later, we want to go even deeper than it seems able to do. We want to have it bring all of our life together, we want to experience what we're seeking in the whole of our lives, and not just in moments of sexuality.

I remember for myself that I have compared great moments of sex (also, I'm working with Joe Kramer in some of the erotic massage) to great moments of religious ritual and great moments of liturgy, when all the senses are rioting, and it's just fullness and wonderful. But sooner or later, there's something in us that wants a cleanness and a dryness, a purity, a desert almost, as we'll see in our next tape, which leads us in a different way, in a way that some of the riot of the senses can't lead us. And as I say, I think this happens in sexuality too, if we are open to it, and if we don't turn around and just seek to recreate the old thrill, which is one of the great dangers in the spiritual life.

We try to recreate the thrill we used to have in religious experience, and in sex we can try and recreate thrills all the time, rather than go through the emptiness into a deeper way of being both spiritual and sexual.

So, the two become one, as I was saying, deeper and deeper as these dark nights are experienced particularly, and we understand viscerally, experientially, in our bodies that there is only one life. This is not a disembodied state, this deep state of fullness of maturity, fullness of spiritual union. The great image of this, of course, is the risen Christ. The risen Christ is a bodily presence. The Gospel writers are at great pains repeatedly to try to point this out in their stories of the apostles seeing the risen Christ, and in their message to the communities they're writing to that there was something very physical and embodied about this new way of living. And that's what it is for us. If we go into the deep places of the spiritual life, we become more embodied, not less embodied, more fully who we are sexually and physically, not less. There is no rejection of the body. And if there has been, and you see this in the mystics, sooner or later, it has to be accepted and embraced anew. It gets caught up in spiritual experience, whether they like it or not, and some of them don't like it, feeling the body is back, and it's back in a new and holy way.

It's interesting to me, for example, that when we look at the story of the woman of Samaria, the woman who went to the well, we find that this woman had had a very checkered sexual background. She'd had at least five husbands and the man she was living with was not her husband. Jesus somehow knows this when he talks to her. And it is to this woman with this very checkered sexual past that Jesus says, 'If you had known who I am, who I was, you would have asked me and I would have given you living water that will become a well within you springing up to eternal life.' It's as if he expects this woman will know something of what he's talking about. It's a fascinating image, the prostitute, or virtually a prostitute, and this man offering the living water, presuming they speak something of the same language; I believe they do. So, this is something of what I would like to suggest is happening when we have sex, when we have a deep sexual life and a deep spiritual life, when we refuse to buy the dualism that we've been sold by our society and our church. I do think though, that there are other things happening when we have sex. As I pointed out at the beginning, I don't think it's this simple.

So, what else is happening when we have sex? What else could be happening when we have sex? Why is it not that simple? Is there some healthy or wise uneasiness that rises up in us when we see some of what goes on in the name of sex, and sometimes in the name of spirituality too? I think it is a very mixed reality. Annie Sprinkle has used the image of sex as food, there being junk food and gourmet food and junk sex and gourmet sex. I would like to extend the metaphor to say there can be junk food sex, there can be wholesome home-cooked-meal type sex, there can be romantic dinner type sex, there can be gourmet sex, and there can be Eucharistic sex, just as there can be all those levels of food. In all of them note please that we are dealing still with food, we are dealing still with sex: the same water, in other words, is flowing through them all. But there are different qualities. Someone who's living their life on junk food or on junk food sex is not going to be all that healthy, and we're not going to feel all that good about a lot of the meals we see them eating. And we would like to tell them there are other ways, more enriching ways, more nourishing ways of doing this. Similarly with sex. Similarly, I might add, with spirituality and religious customs and practices. When we look at some of what passes for religion, some of what passes for spirituality, especially in this culture of the US, we want to say this is junk food. Or even worse, this is positively harmful to the body, not just the individual body, the body of Christ, the body of the world. Some of this stuff is not healthy at all. And personally, I'd feel far more sure saying that about some of what passes for religion than I would about some of what passes for sex, because I do believe there is always something of the true water in whatever sexual practices we have, even in our neuroses, in our pathologies, in our mess, that we're working at in sex, we're still seeking something good, still seeking delight, still seeking the water. Even Aquinas says that when a person commits adultery, what they're seeking in adultery is the delight. They're not seeking the evil, they're seeking the good in adultery, the delight in adultery. I feel it's very true in all of our sex. Fundamentally we're seeking some kind of wholeness, however messed up and mixed up it may be.

When I look at the fundamentalists, I find it hard sometimes to believe that what they are seeking is the true taste of God. In any case, we know that in both these dimensions of our lives, we are experiencing mixed realities. I think one of the things that's happening when we see people having all kinds of sex is that they're seeking the water, but they're mistaking the context for the substance. Remember I was talking about the first time you experienced this, and you feel 'This is it'. There can be a danger that we grab onto the context in which that happens, and we endlessly try to recreate that context with evermore interesting and exotic variations, instead of realizing that what we're seeking is the taste of the pure water, and allowing that longing to lead us deeper and deeper, and let go of the context, that particular context in which we first experienced it. New and more surprising and more enriching ways of experiencing it can open up to us. But we tend to cycle around in a kind of stuck pattern in the same practices, over and over again, and never move deeper.

I think another thing that can be happening when we're having a lot of sex, a lot of different types of sex, is that people are in fact coming to know themselves. They're coming to find, Who am I? What do I want? What do I desire? What happens if I have it? What is going on inside me? And sex is a teacher *par excellence* of this if we really follow it reflectively, and that's the key thing. Remember, I was saying earlier, having mindful pleasure rather than mindless pleasure. If we have mindful pleasure, we can find what our fantasies are, we can find our darkness, we can find the issues around dominance, around submission, issues of power and control, issues of self-destructiveness, issues of compulsivity, issues of obsessiveness, issues of delight, issues of what gives us pleasure, what does nourish us, what does open us; we can find who we are, who is this inside, and sex is a wonderful teacher in this if we explore and use it reflectively.

So, I think a lot of what people are doing in having a lot of sex is finding out who they are. They are asking 'Who am I, what makes me up?' And this is a wonderful and a beautiful thing. It's especially powerful in coming to know our own darkness, who we really are, and what we really are capable of, in all areas, both in the most ecstatic and growth-producing ways, and in the most destructive and dangerous ways, coming to know who I am and find some balance in that. As we know from ancient Greek teachings, and also in all religious teachings, 'know thyself' is an absolutely fundamental maxim of all spiritual life. There can be no knowledge of God unless we come to truly know ourselves, and that means embracing and entering into sex, not denying it and pushing it away. This, of course, can be very unsettling, it doesn't always feel holy, it can feel the opposite. We can feel as if the old self is falling apart, as if who I thought I was is being de-constituted. And that is right on, it is right on, because that's what has to happen to find out who I am, and who it is possible for me to be in the light of God, in the light and the dark of the divine, in tasting this water, and bringing it into myself. If nothing else, it teaches us honesty. And it teaches us to hold our judgments of other people, because we now know who we are too, and what we're capable of. We also know, particularly from the work of Jung, that it is those who have not seen who they are, not seen all they're capable of, who are the most dangerous and the most destructive, because they are repressing facets of themselves and so that stuff will rise up and compel them to behave in all kinds of ways of which they are not in control.

A third thing that can be happening is that people are learning to be comfortable with their bodies. Our bodies, as I was saying earlier, are so divorced from ourselves in this culture, that a lot of this sexual exploration and sexual play, which can go on for years, is learning to be comfortable with my bodily-ness in all of its dimensions. And this is a beautiful and a wonderful thing, how we can be truly erotic with each other. It can also be people just simply seeking play, pleasure, delight, intimacy with other people, other men, other women, just to have the chance to touch and be touched, to feel a communion of bodies. This has been so pushed away from us, so denied us that we can spend years simply trying to redress the balance. And when we find that bodily intimacy, that warmth, whether it's in a hot tub, or in a bed, or in a garden, or in the bushes, when we start to feel some of this intimacy, some of this bodily connection, we want it forever, we don't want to lose it. And why should we? It's our birthright, being holy does not mean that we have to give up plain, beautiful bodily intimacy. So some of this sexual exploration is simply this. You see this also, for example, in young heterosexual men who are having sex with every woman who walks past, or trying to. I think a lot of what they're seeking is touch, is intimacy, and this is the only way they know how to seek it. And sometimes that's true for us. Many of us are going through a kind of adolescence in this as gay men, and just seeking what we never had.

So let's affirm this, let's delight in this. Whenever we feel inclined to judge someone's sexual experiences, however trivial and simple and mechanical they might be (and I'm thinking, for example, of lots of cruising and casual sex, sex in public toilets, sex in the bushes), let's see that these are people seeking something which is fundamentally good and ask ourselves, well, why not? Why not? Why can't this too be something which leads us into the good and the holy? In all of this too, often when we're having sex, we're filling up the hole, we're filling up the emptiness, the loneliness, the pain that we feel. We're facing something of ourselves that is hard to face, and we're experiencing some of its truth and its pain. Now this pain and hurt and loneliness can also feed into our addictions, or compulsions, our obsessiveness, the pain of our incompleteness as human beings. This happens a lot, I think, in sexuality, working out our psychological and emotional shit. And fine, I think that's good. I think that's healthy. I think that can be wholesome, as long as we don't use other people and damage them, as long as we don't get stuck in our own shit, don't get fully compulsive and addicted. If we do, the issue is not the sex, it's the addiction, it's the compulsion, it's the mess that is driving us into that space. And we need maybe to take a break, to breathe and to look at the addictiveness and what the real issue is in our lives, rather than get away from the sex. The sex is not the problem. Just as in a lot of other addictions, the issue is really, What am I seeking? What hole am I seeking to fill up in myself? And to that extent the sex, even a sexual addiction, is a gift, in that it tells us there is something deeply in need here, which must be addressed.

Another thing that can be happening when we're having a lot of sex is we can be avoiding love. We can be avoiding commitments. We can be avoiding the fear of hurt in those experiences. And we can also be at times avoiding the real pain and struggle with spiritual growth. Sometimes the boredom and emptiness that can come in spiritual growth can send us out to have more sex. And I think whenever sex is involved in avoidance, like of love, or of growth or of true spirituality, we have to really think seriously about why am I having this? What is really going on here? So all of this is to say (and we could say a lot more) that no, when we have a lot of sex, we are not simply seeking for the taste of the water of God. There are lots of other things going on too. And we need to look at them very honestly and very reflectively and have mindful pleasure in the midst of them.

This does not mean that they're all not good or that they're therefore not holy; they're holy insofar as they serve to contribute to the wholeness of our growth. I believe that all these different dimensions can in some ways be brought into, and serve, our spiritual journey or growth to wholeness. We don't need to reject and push back any of them. We do need to be mindful and honest and open about what is happening in our sexuality. So, all of this is to say that while a lot of what we're having in sex is not so fantastic, and not so great in some areas, it's also not so terrible either; there was a lot more caring and intimacy and love involved in it than we perhaps at first expected or suspected.

For me, the most powerful evidence of this is the reality of gay men and AIDS. During the 70s, people were having sex like it was going out of style, like it was the end of the world and this was the last chance to have sex. According to what we're told by the church and by some psychologists, and, by the way, by some gay people, this amount of sex and this type of sex should have resulted in us becoming totally dehumanized, becoming very cold, very exploitative, very mechanistic in the way we approached people. Now, what did happen? I'm sure some of that happened but it wasn't the full story. What happened was, AIDS was discovered, AIDS emerged, and of these people who've been having all of this sex, an awful lot of them, have become the most tender, loving, heroic, self-sacrificing, faithful people demonstrating historic love for the church and the world in a way that finds few parallels in human history.

In other words, if we were to make a decision based on that evidence as to what all of this sex produced in terms of human growth, I think we would have to conclude overwhelmingly that it allowed people, when the call came, when the need arose, to be heroically loving, heroically giving. And this is one of the great gifts of gay men, I believe, to our culture.

Two final comments about people who have a lot of sex, about the experience of having a lot of sex in relation to the spiritual life. I was saying that it can teach us self-knowledge. One of the gifts of meditation, of contemplation, of course, is exactly self-knowledge, true self-knowledge, that all our shit comes up. It also comes up in sex if we're open. So I see a very deep parallel there. On a very profound level too, I think one of the great fears we have in having a lot of sex, and in watching people have a lot of sex, and certain types of sex, and experiencing our own desires for lots of sex and certain types of sex, is the fear of losing control, the fear of chaos, the fear of losing myself.

Now, this is exactly the same fear in the depths of the spiritual life, the fear of losing control. And that is exactly what we have to go through. Control is exactly what we have to lose, we have to let go of our lives. Again, I see a deep parallel, and the possibility of one teaching and informing and gracing the other. So for me now, the most profound question that comes up is, given that we can cycle around on the periphery of these two deep rivers, these two deep streams, what will lead us deeper? What will lead us down and draw us down through the water to the place where those two streams become one, where life is tasted at its deepest level, and becomes one and goes underground into the mystery of God? And this is a very profound issue. What is it that will let us drop down, or that will compel us like a salmon upstream? I've spent a lot of time pondering this one. And finally on a beach at Bolinas, (what a beautiful place to be reflecting on this stuff. Bolinas is a coastal area north of San Francisco, a beautiful coastal region) the answer came to me. The contemplative heart is what will draw us down, which is why I've called [these talks] The Erotic Contemplative.

Now what do I mean by a contemplative heart? The contemplative heart is the heart which is able to fully, richly taste and enter into the fullness of everything that can be seen, touched, tasted, felt, experienced with the mind, the body, the senses. It can embrace it richly and fully and enter totally into the full revelation of itself, and of God, in those experiences, whether it's rituals, eucharists, theology, scripture, sexuality, sunsets, oceans, lovemaking, anything that is of the senses and speaks of the Divine, the contemplative heart enters into and tastes it all, vulnerably and fully and says no to none of it. This person is someone fully alive.

The contemplative heart, however, is also totally able to let go of it all, to totally let go of all of that, and say, not that, not that, not that, to realize that anything that can be grasped, or fully tasted or conceptualized, has to be let go of, and the person has to enter into the mystery of God, the silence and the darkness and the stillness, where God is found. Beyond God, there are no words, no images, no senses, no tastes, no sounds, the absolute void, the absolute silence, which I think is at the heart of all religions, and certainly at the heart of Christian mysticism, even though it's often ignored and denied.

Now if a person can do that, can fully taste the beauty and the energy and the joy of all that is sensual and is able to be conceptualized, and at the same time, say 'not that, not that', they get out of this cycle of recreating the context, chasing the thrills, and they can drop down every moment and reach it deeply and have another taste and let go of that, and drop further down, and taste it more deeply and drop further down. Until finally, the tasting and the letting go absolutely become one, in an inarticulable experience of the divine mystery. This is the gift of the contemplative heart. I need to return to this letting go, this 'not that-ing' that doesn't hold or cling to the experience. That's the great danger. This is mine. I have this experience. To let go of it and let the longing (and this is again crucial), let the longing in our heart lead us deeper, let it become our guide. John of the Cross says rather beautifully, 'We will go by night, seeking the fountain of life. Only our thirst is our guide. Only our thirst is our guide.' Never letting what we have experienced tell us that that is the full truth, let our thirsting lead us deeper. As Heidegger said, 'being attentive to the mystery which shows itself and at the same time withdraws, allowing us to follow that withdrawing into silence and letting go.'

I was saying something about not clinging on to the thrills. Now this brings up the issue that I mentioned earlier, which I think is very important, of the danger in sexuality, in spirituality, in life, in drug taking for example, of seeking and clinging to the thrills. Now, in the spiritual life, what we're seeking is a transformed heart, is a totally surrendered being. We are not seeking simply the thrill of spiritual experience, or the thrill of sexual experience. We are seeking to become that which we desire in the deepest level of our being, which is not about a momentary thrill, however holy it might be. For example, Ram Dass, who was experienced in drugs with Timothy Leary, talks about trying to find how the drug experience could become the fullness of life, and how he sought a guru in India to try and give him the LSD to see what would happen. He found one, he gave it to the guru. And the guru simply sat there, took the LSD, continued smiling quietly and didn't change at all. In other words, he already was totally embodying that which the drug momentarily, fragmentarily, gave a sense of.

I also remember that I once gave a group of college students a task: one group to decide what was great sex, the best kind of sex, and the other group to decide what a truly wholly mature person would look like. We brought them back together, and we answered each group's question with the other group's answers. We didn't tell them we were doing that. And what we found was, they were virtually interchangeable. What one group said was great sex was what the other group said were the qualities of a fully mature life in Christ, in God. And that is what we're seeking. But to have that, we have to be able to let go of the momentary thrills and seek the deeper truth.

Now for me, this (talk of momentary thrills) also brings up the issue of long-term monogamy versus casual sex or multiple partners, which are in some ways different, and whether they can be part of the spiritual life. I want to say firstly that in no sense do I in any way denigrate or put down long-term monogamous relationships. I think they are a profound gift to the church and to the world. They are a wonderful model of what true loving is. And there is a kind of growth and development that can happen in those relationships, which perhaps cannot be found anywhere else. I think they are wonderful gifts and holy gifts. But I don't believe that therefore everything else is to be shunned, or regarded as worthless, or as sinful, or as not helping people grow. On the contrary, I believe there are all kinds of ways of growing and living and loving, and all of them can ultimately lead to our growth. Why can't we have both and, rather than either or? Why does the goodness of one have to mean the evil of the other? I don't believe that that is the case at all.

First principle in any of this is telling the truth. The fact is that many of us, most of us, probably have had all kinds of sex in all kinds of situations, or we know people who have. And we've seen that lots of those relationships, however momentary, can be moments of grace, wholeness, and goodness, and can lead us into deep life, and move us forward on the journey. Now we have to tell the truth. Just because it may be respectable in some circles to state that monogamous relationships are the only way (just as it may be fashionable in some circles to call everybody else a slut and pretend that I would never do that, I'm different from that), the fact is that we know from our experience that all kinds of sex can be helpful. Let's own that, let's admit the truth of that, let's reflect on that, let's integrate that, let's find out what that's telling us about life and sex and spirituality, without therefore having to put down people who have long-term monogamous relationships, which is the other side of the coin. Lots of people want to do that too. Let's accept the beauty and diversity of human beings, the beauty and diversity of being together, and the beauty and diversity of spiritual growth.

I would also like to suggest (and this is going out on a limb) that in looking at a theology or spirituality of multiple partners, we could even look at the theology and spirituality of celibacy. Surely it is possible that we can meet together for a brief time, in a spirit of trust, openness and vulnerability, reverencing the other person for who they are beyond the particularities of their ego, where they live, what their name is even, accept our common humanness, enter into a moment of deep shared mutuality, deeply vulnerable loving, experiencing each other at a profound level, experiencing the divine within, giving thanks for that, rejoicing in that, and then bowing and letting each other go, saying, I recognize the God in you, I give thanks, and I let you journey on and I journey on, richer for having been together, and no less rich for parting, which, by the way, is one of the great lines about celibate spirituality, richer for being together, and no less for parting. Could this not also be a model for how we could love, how we could love more than one person, how we could share our lives, even with a lot of people? I need to say, again, I'm talking about a quality of sexual experience, a quality of sexual loving. I'm not simply talking here (I was earlier, but not here) about simple brief encounters in the bushes, I am talking about deeply present, deeply sensual, loving, and I believe it can happen and then be let go of. I think we can do a lot more thinking around a theology of spirituality of this, I think it's very needed.

This brings up the issue of discernment, and this is really where I would like to finish this tape, but I think it's a crucial point. In the mix of all this stuff that I've talked about, around all the kinds of things sex can be and is for different people at different times, long-term monogamy, spirituality, mysticism, multiple partners, all that kind of stuff, how do we discern? How do we discern what is growth, where we're moving, if we are moving, and if we're getting stuck?

I had a dream about three years ago, when I was trying to sort out some of this stuff. And in this dream, I was given three texts: the first epistle of St Paul to the Corinthians, chapter nine, chapter ten and chapter twelve. This was early in the morning, and I thought, what the hell is this, you know? So I waited until I woke up and then went and got the Bible, and I opened up each text. And I'd like to read to you just very briefly what I got from those three chapters: distilled wisdom, I might add, it's not the whole chapter. Some exegetes would disagree with me. What I got was: for me, there are no forbidden things, but not everything does good. True, there are no forbidden things, but it is not everything that helps the building to grow. So, everything is permitted, given basic mutuality, basic respect for the other person, basic care of the humanness of each person, everything is permitted, but not everything is helpful.

So, let's explore, let's play, let's be together, but let's be reflective about what is helping me to move, what is helping me to grow deeper here, what is helping my humanness and what is not, and be prepared to let go of what is not, seeing where I'm getting stuck. That's the first level. The second level of discernment, which indicates where I should be growing, comes from chapter 11. Paul is talking about the Eucharist, and he says, 'Everyone is to recollect himself before eating this bread and drinking this cup, because a person who eats and drinks without recognizing the body is eating and drinking his own condemnation.'

Now, I think the second level of growth is that we are growing to recognize and reverence more and more deeply the God within me and the God within the person that I am making love to. So lovemaking is becoming more and more an act of reverence, and a profound and a holy thing. I at times am overwhelmed with a sense of reverence for you and experience your reverence for me. There are no quick, easy jerk offs in this. This is about really recognizing the divine within one another. And this, I believe, is the second level where we're growing into wholeness as a sexual being.

Interestingly, what Paul is saying here, he's saying because rich people were coming to the Eucharist, eating lavish food and putting the poor people to shame. And Paul was saying, you can't do this, you can't eat of this bread and drink of this cup, and also shame the poor, you must recognize the body. And he means the body of Jesus in the Eucharist, he also means the body of the poor. So I think in this second level, we're also growing to reverence and respect the divine within all people; we're gaining a deeper sense of social justice, a deeper sense of care for the oppressed. And I believe, therefore, our sexual lovemaking should spill over into the way we would treat everyone, especially those who are most rejected, especially those who are most oppressed by our society; this person is becoming a person of justice.

The third level, the deepest level, is one Corinthians 13. I won't read this, we know it pretty well, this is Paul's hymn to love. If I do all kinds of things with my life and have not love, it's a waste of time and energy. This is where we're reaching the communion of love where all of our sexuality and all of our life is tending. This person is coming home, and he's reaching union with the divine. Everything is love, all relationships, all experiences with every being, our love, come from love and lead to love. At this level, I like to say the true saint is someone who could have loving, ecstatic, erotic sex, divine sex with every being and need have sex with none, because they are already living in the fullness of communion of love.

So, this is the deepest level. I think this development of discernment of these three levels is not only linear, it's also circular. These three levels, particularly the first two, with flashes of the deep love coming through, can be happening in our lives at the same time: sometimes our sex is just, it's all permitted but it's not all helpful; sometimes our sex is positively divine in the true sense; and sometimes it's the fullness of the communion of love, beyond even sexuality. But we will gradually be growing more and more to the second level and then to the third level. So I'd like to close with a simple quote from St Paul. After all that's been said, after all that remains to be said (and there is a great deal that remains to be said, I've offered only hints into the mystery, into the exploration that needs to go on), in the end, only three things remain: faith as the response of the whole person, body, mind and heart; hope as that which carries us through the night and the uncertainty and the pain; and love. And the greatest of these is love.

Study Guide

This lecture considers the questions and struggles we face in seeking to integrate our sexuality with authentic Christian spirituality, and explores new models for understanding the interweaving of these energies in our lives:

- What are the conversations we are afraid to have regarding sex?
- Is sex 'good'? Does it need to be 'justified'? The importance of 'suspecting grace'.
- The integration of sexuality and spirituality—are they the same energy?
- 'Tasting the Water' in sexuality and spirituality:
    - The first taste
    - The mystery that shows itself and at the same time withdraws
    - The heart's desire: being drawn 'upstream'
    - The Desire is One; the Water is One
    - Going 'underground' towards the Source.

- Qualities of deep sexual experience mirroring qualities of deep spiritual experience.
- Pleasure—its power, our fear.
- We come alive, long to go deeper, become open:
    - Deep sexual experience begins to merge with the spiritual
    - Deep spiritual experience begins to merge with the sexual
    - The dark night of the soul; the dark night of sex?
    - The One life of God

Yet, it is not so simple. What else may be going on in sexual desire/activity?

- Seeking depth but mistaking context for substance
- Coming to know myself

- Coming to know my body
- Filling the 'hole' within myself
- Avoiding love, commitment, growth
- Mindless pleasure versus mindful, heartfelt pleasure.
- Does 'promiscuous' sexual activity 'dehumanise' us?
- Sex as teacher: the fear of losing control; self-knowledge
- What will take us into the depths? The Contemplative Heart.
- Living the experience: the part longs to become the whole
- Multiple partners and long-term monogamous relationship—could there be a place for both in spiritual development over a lifetime?

Discernment: towards the new model.

*

Various quotes in this lecture about the powerful spiritual energies and transcendent experiences that may be present in sexual ecstasy and orgasm come from an essay by Mary D. Pellauer: 'The Moral Significance of Female Orgasm: Toward Sexual Ethics That Celebrates Women's Sexuality' in the *Journal of Feminist Studies in Religion*, Vol. 9. No. 1/2 (Spring–Fall 1993), pp. 161-182.

Questions for discussion and reflection

1. What is the conversation about sexuality that you, as an LGBTIQ+ Christian, most feel the need for?

2. Is sex 'good'? What qualifications or criteria for discernment would you like to add? Do you feel at ease with the idea of sex as inherently good, not needing justification? Why or why not?

3. 'The Mystery that shows itself and at the same time withdraws'. When have you experienced this in your own life?

4. Have you ever experienced sexual desire or sexual relating as deeply spiritual? Did this affect your prayer life and your relationship with and understanding of God?

5. How do you see the Church's attitude to sexuality? Why do you think that Christianity has had such a difficult time with sex? How has this affected you personally? Does it still affect you?

6. 'If I'm enjoying myself, it must be wrong'. Do you ever feel guilty about pleasure? Do you feel that you must limit the amount of pleasure you let into your life? Where do these feelings and ideas come from? What might liberate you to delight more fully and freely in your God-given body and your capacity for sensual pleasure?

7. 'Sex, including our sexual desires and fantasies, can be a great teacher'. What has sex and sexual desire taught you about yourself? About life? About God? About authentic spirituality?

8. How does a person 'deepen' their sexual experience? How does a person 'deepen' their spiritual experience? How do you?

9. Multiple partners and spirituality: what do you think about this issue? What do you feel about it? How have these thoughts and feelings been formed? How do you feel about being open to new questions and explorations in this whole area?

10. In re-visioning sexuality, especially from the perspective of spiritual growth, what discernment points would you consider important? How does one discern that which leads to authentic growth, and that which hinders it?

3

Exodus and Awakening

So welcome to our third session in this series. This session is entitled 'Exodus and Awakening', and in this time together, we hope to consider two of the most important, the most crucial, the most central themes in Christian spiritual life, and indeed, in all life, and especially in gay life. They are the themes of exodus, of leaving, of liberation, of coming out in some sense; and the theme of coming alive, of awakening. So, before we begin, let's just take a moment of silence together. As I speak, I'm aware that, again, although we're separate in time and space, part of our liberation, part of our freedom is to realize that in truth, there is no separation. So let's be quiet and silent together for a moment, and let the spirit speak in our hearts.

And may the light and the love of the Holy Spirit be in our heart and on our lips.

Amen.

*

This theme of Exodus, this theme of waking up and of moving out, is at the very heart of the spiritual life, and of the Christian understanding of what it means to come alive. And as always, whenever we talk about anything to do with coming into maturity as a Christian, we see things in terms of the death and the resurrection of Jesus. The death and resurrection of Jesus always has to be the central motif, the central paradigm, the central way we understand who we are, and who we're coming to be, as Christians, as human beings. At the same time, from the earliest times in the church's history, there's been a need to tell stories, to find ways of reflecting or enfleshing the death and resurrection of Christ. What does it mean to live this out in a real life, in a human life? To find these stories, one of the first places that the early Christians looked was the Old Testament, which makes sense since most of these people were originally Hebrews. These were the great stories of their childhood, of their youth, of their mature lives, the great stories that had led them to some sense of being God's people. And the essential story in the whole of the Old Testament, the essential story for Israel, of course, is always the Exodus, the liberation from Egypt. One of the crucial things about Exodus is that Jews were always asked to remember that God freed them from Egypt, it was not just your ancestors 2000 years ago, but rather, you were brought out of Egypt. And similarly for us, the themes we talk about, whether it's the Exodus or the death and resurrection of Christ, are meaningless unless they take flesh in our lives and in our bodies. There's no point in having a notional assent to them, or the assent of faith, if they're not lived out. One of the great mystics of the western tradition, Meister Eckhart, once said, 'What good is it to me if the Virgin Mary gave birth to Christ 2000 years ago, if she does not also give birth to Christ in me, in my time, in my life, in my space.' With that theme in mind—that we need to enflesh these stories in our lives—we go forward.

When we look at the story of Exodus, we find that it begins with a call of God. Everything in Scripture, everything in the movement of the spiritual life, is fundamentally God's initiative. And this call, which comes to the people of Israel, living in slavery in Egypt, harks back to an earlier call that we need to look at briefly first, and that's the call of Abraham, which is the great paradigm for any call in Judeo-Christian history. The call of Abraham is addressed to this man who was then Abram, who was not a Hebrew, who was not one of the people of Yahweh; they didn't really exist yet. Suddenly, this call came to him when he was quite old, living an ordinary life like the people around him, quite a prosperous life. And the call was this. It comes from Genesis 12. 'Yahweh said to Abram, leave your country, your family, and your father's house, for the land that I will show you. I will make you a great nation. I will bless you and make your name so famous that it will be used as a blessing. I will bless those who bless you, I will curse those who curse you. All the tribes of the earth shall bless themselves by you. So Abraham went, as Yahweh told him.' This beautiful simple example of the call has been used over and over again through the centuries and continues into our day as the seminal call, which leads us forward. And the call that you'll notice is leave, leave, get out, go. Leave your family, leave your country, leave your father's house, for the land that I will show you.

Remember that Abraham was living quite a successful life with lands and tribes and servants and sheep and goats, quite prosperous for his time. And he was asked to leave and move out, without maps, without details; Yahweh did not go on to say, 'Go here and then go there, and turn left down by the 711, and take a right by the bridge'. It was just 'leave'. That reminds me of something the poet Machado said: 'Traveler, there is no path, paths are made by walking'. So the call is to walk, to leave, to move, to get out, and to go with a simple trust that somehow in some way, the promise will be fulfilled. We see this too in the Exodus, (and we'll talk in more detail later) when the people leave Egypt to enter the wilderness with no maps and no guides except Moses, who didn't really know where he was going himself, just trusting that somehow God was leading them.

We also see it in a very strange group of wild men, in the early centuries of the church's history (and women too I might add; we tend to always think of these particular people as being men, but many of them were not, there were women who did the same thing, moved the same way). These were the desert monks, desert nuns, and just as we look to the Old Testament for our stories of how to enflesh the death and resurrection of Christ, to reclaim these stories as our own, we can also look to the great stories of Christian tradition, of

Christian history, and reclaim them as our own as well. Since liberation is not something that just happens to us, it's been happening down through the centuries to others, and we can learn from them.

These people lived in about the third and fourth centuries, probably more the fourth century, at a time when Christianity was becoming more and more popular, more and more the 'thing'. It was becoming the state religion. Gradually it was moving from a situation where if you were Christian your life was at stake, to a situation where if you wanted to get on, particularly get on in politics, you needed to be a Christian (it's starting to sound familiar, isn't it?). Even nominally, just to be able to use the name, that was the way you would make it. It was also a society that was crumbling; its structures, its sense of meaning, its moral codes, its sense of values, were falling apart. It was under attack from barbarian tribes, as they were termed then, and it was literally beginning to collapse. These men and women left the cities, went out into the desert and began to live lives of silence and prayer and a lot of harsh penance, often very much alone, seeking a purer, deeper kind of Christianity. And often, they left with a sense of urgency, as if the world around them was somehow seducing them into a kind of slavery, as if to stay would in some ways put their life at stake. And so often they really fled. It was a fleeing of the cities and of this very bourgeois kind of Christianity that had become the state thing, the way to get on in life, to find what they saw as the martyrdom of the desert. Just as the martyrs put their lives on the line, so these people wanted to put their lives on the line too. They wanted that kind of Christianity. So they fled a very particular kind of a world, a very corrupt, compromised kind of a world that was losing its way.

It reminds me too, for example, of Francis of Assisi in the 13th century. Again, quite a rich, successful young man who had a wonderful career in front of him, and Francis too left, left all of that, and became a beggar, went out from the city to live in the forests and in caves, and gradually found a new way of being Christian, which has revitalized and inspired people for the last 800 years and is still inspiring people today. That's the power of this call to leave. It inspires people down the centuries, it's not just for oneself.

And when I talk about people leaving, people fleeing, people leaving their father's house, leaving their country for another land, I think about gay people, and the very many gay people who in very literal senses have left their father's house, their towns, their states, their countries, to another land, to find another place where they can, in some sense, be themselves, where we can be ourselves. The classic stories, for example, of people fleeing places like the Midwest in the United States, to go to San Francisco, or to New York, or to Amsterdam, or maybe to London, or maybe to Sydney, people fleeing often tiny rural towns, hoping that in the cities they might find a different freedom, a different way of being themselves. Often there also is this sense of urgency of our lives being at stake, or certainly our sanity being at stake, and the impulse from within driving us to get out, leave; the only way to find life is to leave and find freedom somewhere else.

When I look at the kind of world that gay people are leaving when they do this, I think of the world the monks left. This term 'world', it's a difficult one, because so often the world and the spirit have been opposed to each other, and that's not true, of course, everything is saturated with spirit. When 'world' is used in this sense, it brings a very particular kind of human reality, a human reality that is very much enslaved to greed, to rampant ambition, to exploitation of people, of the earth, of oneself, of religion, subjecting everything to gods of mammon, money, power, prestige, the status quo, the structures that uplift some and enslave the many. That's the kind of world we're talking about, that demands people be a certain way, so that things can be a certain way for certain people. And you get on by becoming one of those people and obeying their rules, and everyone else is at the bottom, as kind of serfs, to support this structure. That is what's meant by leaving the world in this context.

Maybe it's not such a bad kind of world to leave. I really believe that whether we're looking at Abraham or the desert monks or gay people in our time, we are looking at the call of the divine lover, the call of God, the call of the Spirit, however we want to image that reality, coming up from within us and impelling us to move, not to stay in our so-called security, but to get out. And it's God's initiative, not our own. I firmly believe that; we respond to a call.

It's also a call to find my people, to find a place of belonging. And here I'm aware of how often we feel that we have no people, we are no people. It's in this experience that we become a people, as we'll see happened to Israel. Always, the issue is freedom, freedom, freedom! There is nothing that is more at the heart of what Christian life is about than freedom. And so of course, it's a great pain to me, and I'm sure to many of us, to see what is done in the name of Christianity, right through the centuries but particularly in our time. The call is one of freedom. Let's not have that call polluted, distorted or taken away from us. So, leave and let go.

I'd like to turn now to Moses, to the great story of the Exodus, which is the theme of this particular session.

Let's just recall the situation for a moment, for those of us who perhaps haven't read the book of Exodus for quite some time, which is probably quite a few of us. We have a situation where the people of Israel, the Hebrews, were not a very specific group of people in some ways at this period. They were a very motley group of slaves and oppressed people, the Habiru, who lived in Egypt, and had been there for a long time, perhaps captured in the desert, wandering nomads, taken into slavery, and had been there for a long time, probably some hundreds of years.

Gradually, the oppression gets worse and worse; they're pressed into slavery, building the great cities, maybe the pyramids. Whether this happened historically, we're not sure, but certainly this is the great story. Finally, the oppression gets particularly acute because they're breeding a great race, and the Egyptians are frightened that the slave population will overtake them in numbers. So, the Egyptians begin to throw their firstborn sons into the Nile River. And it's at this point, when the oppression has become this acute, that God sends Moses, calls Moses and then sends Moses. Moses, who is himself a Hebrew, comes back into the land of Egypt after a time of purification in the desert, encountering God, and his great call to the gods of Egypt and to the Pharaoh of Egypt is 'let my people go'. So we have 'leave', and we have 'let my people go'. Moses comes in to really say two things: one, my people are in slavery, and two, let them go. And both of these things are really crucial.

The first part is to recognize and to realize when we are in slavery. And this is probably the most crucial moment in the life and growth of the gay and lesbian person, to realize what is being done to us, what has been built into our bones almost from the time before we were born even. The messages, the conditioning, the programming, the oppression that has gone on, right from the sort of images and dreams that our mother and father may have had when we were in the womb, that we would be a certain way, that our lives would go along certain paths. And that has become part of who we are.

At the same time, we have started to realize or suspect or fear that maybe we are not that way. And for 15, 20, 25, 30, 45, 50, 60 years sometimes, we have oppressed and kept down who we are because of what has been done to us, what has been told to us. As we've grown, we've started to realize this is not just a way of saying 'this is the way you should be', it's a way of saying 'you'd better be this, or your life is at stake, your life, your sanity, your jobs, your future career, your prosperity, your physical wellbeing, your respect, your prestige in the culture'. And again, very literally, in many cases, 'your life'. If you are not this way, if you don't abide by these rules and behave in this way, your life is not only not going to be worth living, you may not have a life. And we pick this up very, very quickly, very early.

I listen to my little nieces and nephews, who are seven or eight, back in Australia. I don't know if it's happening here, but 'gay' has become a term to say, 'Oh, that's really stupid', 'Oh, that sucks' or 'that's really dumb'. They'll say, 'oh, gee, that's gay'. And you might pull them up on it. They say 'no, we don't mean anything, we don't mean it's bad to be gay'. But this is the word that's being used even in 1994. We know this, all this stuff goes into us, right from the time we begin to understand what speech means or even just to pick up what terms mean. And then to wonder, could I be this? Might this be me? I think of my mother at times saying things about queers. You know, I confess, I still find that word a little difficult because of the way it was used, and the bewilderment, not knowing what she meant, but the kind of subtle feeling, maybe she's talking about me. And sometimes she was a little more specific, or hinted at it a little more strongly, as this was not a thing to be. We take in all this stuff, and we start to become or pretend or act as if we are what the society demands we be.

So, we become enslaved to our families. We become enslaved very much to the society around us that does not want us to be who we are, does not want anything to change. And if we become who we are, brother, sister, things are going to change. We become enslaved to the church, which in its most gracious moments tells us, it's okay to be who we are, as long as we don't act on it. Like, don't live, don't breathe, don't have a body, don't have a sexuality. Just kind of be a condition, be an orientation, don't be a person. And so often we take this on, and we struggle. Just last night, I was talking to a man of fifty, a beautiful, wise man who practices yoga as a yoga teacher but who grew up in a very traditional black, gospel-oriented family, and in jest he said, 'Well, who knows, what if the God at the end of our lives turns out to be the God of hellfire, and maybe that's where we're all going, haha.' It's still there. It's still there, inside us.

This slavery is not something that's thrown off easily. So we become enslaved to the church. Often, we serve the church. I often wish that all gay people in the church would strike for three days, I mean, all churches, all denominations, go on strike for three days and watch the place fall apart. Because we make the thing run; as someone from the Catholic tradition, I certainly know that that's true. I also know it's true in the Episcopal Church. And I'm sure it's true in very many ways for all the other denominations as well. We are often the people who bring a deep sense of the spiritual, a deep commitment, a deep creativity, a deep self-giving, a deep devotion to the church. We accept the slavery ourselves, become enslaved to the church. We also become enslaved to 'myself', and this is slightly more subtle and more complicated because this is the kind of slavery that in our spiritual tradition we talk about the most. It's the slavery to the values of the world we talked about, a slave to comfort, security, to getting on, to being seen as okay in other people's opinions, a slave to my own sense of who I am, that I have a certain role in society.

I think of a wonderful scene in *Angels in America*, where Roy Cohn basically says (he's just been told he has AIDS by his doctor and the doctor implies he may be a homosexual), 'Homosexuals are people who have no clout. I have clout, therefore I cannot be a homosexual, therefore I cannot have AIDS.' The sense of self, 'I have clout, therefore I can't be one of these people'. Denying who he was absolutely. Denying it so totally that he oppressed other people who were the same tribe, because he couldn't face the slavery within himself. He'd sold himself into slavery. And this is often the hardest slavery to really address.

Now, these combined slaveries, these combined slave masters of family, of society, of church and of ourselves can not only attack us individually or enslave us individually, they can present this incredibly united front. So that family is saying the same thing, our society is saying the same thing, our church is saying the same thing, and most of all our selves, our superego if you like, is saying the same thing. And there is this poor, apparently weak little voice inside saying, 'I don't think so. I don't really think so.' It's like this little boy or little girl up the back of the class tentatively putting up their hand and saying, 'Excuse me! Bullshit. This is not true.' And that frightened, often fragile little voice, that is the voice of freedom. That is the voice that hears the call of the Holy Spirit to come out, to leave, to let my people go. That is the voice we have to look for. That is the voice we have to listen to, that's the still small voice, which is the voice of God, not in the earthquake, or in the storm or in the fire, as the prophet Elijah experienced it, but in the still small voice, which says, 'This, isn't it! This is not it! Move, freedom awaits you. Come out, come forward'!

This command of God (it's not just an invitation) to 'let my people go', is addressed in the Scriptures to the Pharaoh, but it's also addressed to the gods of Egypt. Yahweh says again and again, I will make judgments, I'll pass judgment on all the gods of Egypt, and I will conquer the gods of Egypt. So these are the gods that I've spoken of, these are the gods of this kind of comfort, this kind of security, this kind of ambition, this kind of structural enslavement that wants nothing to change, that wants some people to rise and some people to support them by their lives, by their oppression, by their slavery. These gods are the gods that the God, the One, wants to pass judgment on, and is saying, 'Let my people go'.

But these gods are not just outside us, they're also inside us. And before my people are going to be let go, there's going to be a mighty struggle that goes on here. It's not going to be an easy process. And I say this to gay and lesbian people who have come out, who I'm sure realize, as we all do, these gods don't let go that easily. No, they're in our guts, folks. And they're gonna keep up the battle as long as they can. So we have this wonderful story in the Scripture. These gods feel their sense of power and control being threatened, as they sense judgment being passed on them. In some sense our freedom says that they're full of shit, and their bluff is called. We have the story of the 10 plagues. Pharaoh wouldn't let the people go, so Yahweh sent 10 plagues, really terrible plagues of frogs and lice and all kinds of things.

The waters turned to blood and day turned to darkness and all sorts of horrible things happened. And after each plague, Moses went back to Pharaoh and said, 'Well, you're going to let them go now?' And Pharaoh would say, 'No, no, no, no, no.'

So what I see is this tussle. We start to feel the struggle in our guts, in our bones, we start to feel the slavery, we start to feel the oppression. And there's movement to get out, to move towards freedom. But no, no, no, the gods aren't going to let us go yet. Our family says, well just keep it quiet, just don't tell the neighbors, just don't make a fuss. Our friends say, well, yeah, we understand, but you know, don't tell anybody at work, don't do anything foolish. Our church says, well, yeah, but you know, don't have sex, and then don't tell anyone in the church around you that you're, you know, like that. Our society says, well, you know, yes, but no marriage, don't demonstrate in the streets, just go to work and be quiet and be like everyone else. Don't do anything in the street and frighten the horses. There's this tussle, and this voice inside gets stronger, saying, 'I've got to be free. I've got to be free. This isn't it. This isn't it.' So I see this as the 10 plagues.

I'll have to say this, there's this wonderful part of us, well, wonderful/dreadful part of us. I think of *Murder in the Cathedral*, a wonderful play by TS Eliot, based on the true story of Thomas Beckett in the 12th century. He was an archbishop, long story, had a major fight with the king, and he's been in exile in France, and he's coming back to London. And the people know there is going to be trouble, big trouble. And in fact, Thomas ends up being stabbed to death by the king's knights in his own Cathedral. Well, the people have some sense of this. And when he's coming back (he's the archbishop), they're in the streets saying, 'Thomas, Archbishop, go back to France'. We have lived these seven years or so living and partly living, living and partly living. And there have been births and deaths and marriages and plagues and famines, but we've gone on living, living and partly living. We do not want anything to happen.

And that's the cry of these gods within us. We do not want anything to happen. We don't want anything to change. It's been okay. We've been living, living and partly living—but living! We've gotten by, just keep it quiet. These are the gods that are being challenged.

Now, part of the problem too is not just these gods not wanting to let us go, it's the fear of the wilderness, the sense that on the other side of leaving, on the other side of letting go, what is there?

What is there if we do come out? Freedom? What's it going to look like? What's it going to taste like? What will happen? My God, what will happen? How do I make a living, how will everyone react? This need to know what the geography will look like of this new land. And into the midst of that there is the voice of God saying, 'Trust me, the land I will show you, trust me, come out, come forward, leave.' It's scary. The cost is very great, the cost of the contemplative life and spiritual life, it's very great. The monks who left their homes and went to the desert lived very poor and rough lives. Very often lonely lives. In the gay movement, in gay moving out, in moving out into freedom as gay and lesbian persons, we know the costs can be enormous. It's important that we take this seriously. I mean, not everyone lives in The Castro, thank God. Even those who do know that the cost is very real; in other places in the world, it can be far more devastating. So it gives us pause. It's wise to wait and to look and to be cautious, and to smell the change, and smell the possibilities and be aware of our fears. Don't move until the time is right. So the struggle goes on.

What finally moves us, what finally gets us out? In Exodus, it's the death of the firstborn. Finally (terrible story in some ways) Yahweh, at wit's end, strikes down the firstborn sons of all of the Egyptians. And that forces Pharaoh to say, 'Get the hell out of here. Get these people out of here', and they leave. So, he lets them go. What is this death? What is this death? How can we interpret this?

This is what allows the exodus to take place in the story. If we're going to make the story ours, how do we understand this? Not easy. I think it's the death of the future. Your firstborn son, especially in that kind of a society, was the inheritor. Okay, he was the guarantee of the clan, the family, continuing, carrying on the genetic code we would say now, but certainly he was the promise for the future. His death is the death of the future. I think what moves us out is the death of the future.

With the monks, they started to realize that the society that they were living in was killing them. It promised lots of goodies; quite a lot of these people were quite secure, quite well-off people. They were often educated people who fled the cities into these harsh Syrian deserts to live these extraordinary lives, and I might add, to leave us extraordinary wisdom in the mystical tradition. They could have had very comfortable lives in many, many cases. But there was a sense that there is no life for me here anymore. This is killing me. The future, as I understood it, has died, it's dead. I have to get out and find some other possibility. I can't stay in the tension any longer, I've got to get out. This is killing me.

For gay Christians, I think the death of the firstborn is the death of the church. It's the realization there is no future for me in this community. Now, I don't necessarily mean that in an absolutely literal sense, because the true community, the true people of God, the true church is my true home. But in this community, in this version, in this structured version of the church, this thing that calls itself church and often isn't, this group of people, this institution that I have often given so much of my life and so much of my heart and soul to, there is no life for me. There is no future for me anymore. And so the church dies. And the pain is so great that it forces me out the gates, through the waters and on the journey.

That's the death of the firstborn, I think, for a gay Christian. I can't think of anything that is much more painful. Because as I say, this is like our flesh and blood. This is like our bones. This is who we are, this is our heart. And in some sense, to follow the call of God, to follow the call of the divine love into freedom, we have to leave the very community that first led us into some awareness of God, and of God's love. And that's an intensely painful and challenging thing to do.

I think of cases, for example, in O'Neil and Ritter's wonderful book *Coming out Within*. One case of a sister who had worked all her life in the church, and one Sunday listening to a sermon (she'd come to realize she was lesbian), she suddenly realized, listening to this man up there, that there was no place for her as a woman, and certainly as a lesbian; that this community she had devoted her life to did not want her as she was.

I remember for myself, the first time I sat in a church and realized, this institution that I have given so much of my life to does not want me to go to the table, does not want me to receive the Eucharist. And not only that, but most of the actual people in this church, if they knew who I was, they wouldn't want me to go to the table either.

So there's a kind of a death, and one is forced to move. This journey is also often symbolized as the second journey, as the journey that often happens, say, in midlife for a lot of people. Jung talks about this a lot, that we reach a point in our lives where we realize the old story can't do it anymore. It falls apart. Sometimes it's losing a job, or becoming sick, or having a divorce, death of a child, death of a spouse, all kinds of things that are forced on one; we don't choose this, the journey is too painful. We have too much invested in the status quo. We don't just say, 'Oh, I think I'll live a totally different life from today'. This is forced onto us, but given that it is, we later realize the gift and the blessing that this, what seemed like a catastrophe at the time, has been. For a lot of people, this experience of the death of the future, when they realize that they're gay and lesbian, only later comes to be seen as a great gift, a great call of freedom. But I'd still say it's not necessarily something we choose. In this context, AIDS has been very much a call into this journey for a lot of people, both those who've had AIDS, or have AIDS, and those who minister, care for people with AIDS, and also people with HIV. The realization that life is different now, the realization of mortality, the realization of one's exile, one's stigma in society, the realization that the gods of gay culture aren't going to support one very much through this journey, the realization that life is limited, forces people onto a different kind of journey. This too is an exodus. So I see AIDS, with all its horror, as in some ways a gift as well, as every tragedy, every turning point can be.

Sometimes the real exodus comes only after we have in a sense come out, whether that's coming out within or outside or both, and I'll talk a little bit about that in a moment. It comes afterwards when we start to share the story with other people, and we start to realize what we've done. We start to see their reactions and feel their estrangement, their 'Oh, aah, you sure?' And we start to realize, 'Oh my God, I've just come out, I've just moved, I've just left, I've just let my people go'. And sometimes it's that pain and that sense of rejection, of estrangement, which really is the exodus for us. In any case, somewhere in some way, the gods, the gods of Egypt begin to let us go, we begin to respond to the call to leave, we begin to move out.

In the story, you may be wondering what happened in Exodus, those of us who don't know it that well, or haven't seen Cecil B DeMille for some time. What happens next is that the people are led out by a pillar of fire at night and a pillar of cloud by day, beautiful images. In this journey that we make, I see them as passion, fire. Our passion leads us forward. And the pillar of cloud is a sense of mystery, of unknown and of new possibilities, that lead us forward, that are our guiding points as we move out of the land of slavery.

They also go through the waters. They get to the Reed Sea, or the Red Sea, and think how the hell are we gonna get through this? And they're being pursued by Pharaoh and his chariots. Pharaoh, who just changes his mind at the last minute and chases them. These gods, as I say, don't want to let us go. They want slaves to keep making the bricks to build the cities (you know, we've been doing that all our lives, hey, let's take a break. Let's do it differently, but the gods don't want to let us go), so they give chase. The people are between the sea and Pharaoh, and Moses stretches out his hand, the waters part and they go through. Pharaoh and his chariots chase them. The people get through, then Moses stretches out his hand and the waters flow back and they're all drowned. Like a lot of stories in the Old Testament, this one is a little bit gory. It's still a good story. The people are free on the other side of the water. What does this say? What is this about for us in our Exodus?

I can only speak personally, I suppose. I think this is sort of like that point you get to when you think, 'This is not going to work. I've blown it. I've come out. How the hell am I going to get through this?' Somehow the territory looks impassable. It looks like there is no way through, no way to a new kind of life. And somehow, in some way, we get through the waters. Maybe it's just with the help of some friends, reading the right book, saying the right prayer, having some sense that it's okay, it's gonna be alright, or just a word of encouragement from someone. Sometimes it's going to a new place and finding that there is a new way of being. Sometimes it's finding a group of people who can be community for us.

But always, it seems to me, there is initially a sense that I'm not going to get through it. And yet we do. And that 'getting through' is the waters parting. Somehow we find ourselves on the other shore, and we look back and we think, 'How the hell did I ever live back there?' From the other side it looks like that was not life at all. But before we enter the waters, when the sea appears as a barrier, there is the question, "What the hell do I do now?" Trust and go forward, and the waters will part. That's our trust, that's our call. That's the promise that we will be led, where there is no path, where it seems impossible to go. So we pass through the waters and we come to the other side. And here there is a great and solemn joy. And if there isn't, there damn well ought to be. If there isn't, we'd better ask ourselves, what the hell's going on? Not that everything's happy, happy, happy. There is a great and solemn joy.

I'd like to read you a very simple little passage from Exodus. Some scholars say that these couple of lines are amongst the very oldest in Scripture, from a very ancient oral tradition. Miriam the prophetess, Aaron's sister, and Moses' sister, took up a timbrel, and all the women followed her with timbrels, with tambourines, dancing, and Miriam led them in the refrain, singing, 'Sing of Yahweh, he has covered himself in glory, horse and rider he has thrown into the sea.' And that's it. Just those couple of lines, later made into a long, epic song. Just sing of Yahweh, he's covered himself in glory, he's drowned the gods of Egypt and their minions in the sea. The waters of our passing through, the waters of our baptism, if you like, into a new life, the waters of our freedom, has drowned the gods of Egypt, the gods of slavery and oppression. So, hey, rejoice. It's important to say that this exodus takes place in a community. It's not just done alone. And we'll talk a little bit about that at the end of the talk.

So, I want to consider now with you, how is it that we heard the call? How does it come to us, this call of liberation? How is it experienced? How do we come to realize that we were in slavery? And also what is it that makes it worth the insecurity, the struggle, the pain, the alienation, the loss of so much of our lives and our sense of self as we come out. And I stress again that I'm talking both about coming out within, to our souls, and to our God, however we image God, but also about coming out in a more public sense. I do believe that for different people in different times, those two things are appropriate. Personally, I believe absolutely that we are all called gradually in our journey to a public coming out, however and whenever that takes place. And I really do believe that coming out can be incarnated for different people in different ways. I have absolutely no doubt that every single one of us is called to come out inside, to come out to ourselves, to own who we are, and to own that in the presence of our God. To hear the words of letting go, of freedom, of acceptance, of promise addressed to us as gay and lesbian people. Until that has happened, no amount of coming out publicly is true coming out, is true freedom. It's the gods within that keep us in slavery—that's the real slavery.

So how does this awakening, how does this call come? I just gave you the word. It comes as an awakening, waking up. And this is a core concept in all understandings of the spiritual life. Buddha was supposed to have been asked once by someone, are you a god? And Buddha said, 'I'm awake, I'm awake.' That's the answer, to wake up. And when one is awake, the rest of life as it *was* lived is like sleep, like being in a coma, like being in a closet, shut in, unable to smell the daisies, unable to breathe fresh air, unable to hug and embrace ourselves and one another. So this awakening … in contemplative life, in spiritual life, there are two awakenings, before the exodus and after the exodus. Before the exodus, before the moving out (and I think of the pattern of those early monks, leaving the cities, as a great pattern of spiritual life), there's an awakening of spiritual joy. What before was routine and simply 'words' suddenly comes alive with juice and beauty. Suddenly the words of Scripture just set us on fire. We experience the sweetness, the taste, and see that God is good. We experience this as, 'my God, this is real, this is alive, I can taste it, the juice, the sweetness'. And the other side of that (and there's always another side, as you may have gathered) is awakening to the deadness, to the routine, to the numbness, to the hypocrisy, to the double dealing, both within myself and around me. We can't be blind to it any longer.

Now that sets us on the journey, sets us on the exodus in the spiritual life. And you know, there's pain and there's dryness and there's joy and there's compromise and there's freedom and there's struggle. And somehow we come out, somehow we leave, and for these early monks, it was leaving the cities in a very literal sense. For many of us, it's a different kind of leaving, it's like true conversion of heart, when we actually do choose different gods. Up until now we've been struggling, and somehow at this point, we do choose different gods. And it is a leaving of the old gods, the old values, the old ways by which we named our lives and ourselves. And we come out and we discover the most beautiful thing, the fresh air, that there is a new life on the other side that we hardly dreamed about.

For me personally, this happened a number of years ago when, after teaching for thirteen years, I literally dropped out and went and lived on the beach for a year. And mixed in with all the pain and the loneliness and the shit of that year, there was this fresh air, there is a life here that I hardly knew existed, hidden, which you only taste when you come out, when you leave. That's the second awakening. And the downside of it, a deeper downside, is there is no way back. Once you've tasted this life, you ain't never going back. And it's not always beautiful. It's not always wonderful. At times, you think you're crazy, and you've just lost it, and you ought to chuck all this and go and get a proper job, have a proper life, make some real money, as my mother says, find a real husband, wife, children, home, mortgage, whatever. And by the way, this new life can be found in the midst of all of those, if we're truly free.

For me, it wasn't. For those early monks it wasn't. But hey, this is life, this is free, and this is fresh air. Why would I go back there? And being true to that is part of the struggle. There'll be more exoduses and more struggles, more freedoms, more goings out, but these two are core: the awakening to spiritual joy; and the awakening to a new life on the other side of exodus. Sometimes it's gradual and sometimes it's an earthquake. In fact, an earthquake is a good image of it. There's this movement under the ground, the plates are grinding, the tension's building, and then there's this slip, and we're on the other side. We only got there by all this gradual grinding and struggle, and then this freedom. So the earthquake is a good image for that. Sometimes we're aware of the earthquake, and sometimes we're aware of the grinding and the struggle that leads up to it. But you need them both.

I want to compare these two awakenings in the spiritual life with two awakenings for gay people. I love this part. Firstly, it's the awakening that our sexual desires are okay, that it's all right to love men, to be turned on by men, that it's all right if we're lesbian to be turned on by women, it's okay. It's maybe even good. And we actually start to feel this and start to own the fact that I do feel this, I do get turned on by men, and hey that's all right. Oh, my God, what a transition. After all the shit that's been loaded on us, for one poor, scared, frightened person to say, 'It's okay'. That little voice. I mean, God, that's leaping mountains, to be able to say that in our society. So that's the first awakening.

The downside of it is that we feel more deeply the pain and the contradiction of feeling what we've been told we're not to feel, and that we've taken on. And that's the downside, we feel that far more acutely. And we feel the fear and the uncertainty that we're stepping outside the bounds. We're crossing over. We're breaking the law. That's scary. I refer back to my story in the first session of both feeling the joy of sexual encounter, and feeling that everything in me wanted to say this was bad, but I knew it wasn't. And the wrench of that, that's part of the pain of this awakening.

The second awakening, which is in some ways far more profound but can't happen unless the first one happens, is the awakening of sexuality as holy, as grace, as divine, as saturated with the love and the presence of God: the realization this is not just good and okay, this is sacred, this is the way into the divine itself. This is the love of God coming to meet me, coming alive in me. This is not just all right, this is divine. And to be in the life of God is to live fully with this. This is the second awakening. This is the true and deepest awakening. And after this, there is no turning back. There is no turning back. We have really gone through the waters.

I'd like to recite a poem for you that I think expresses this very beautifully. It's a poem that I wrote, when this first happened for me, the first time I was with another man and felt in my guts the holiness of this, which would not be denied. I'd like you to perhaps close your eyes or to go within yourself, and to hear this in your own experience.

We have built a fire
In the black fireplace, tonight
A change
Its fingers laugh at the logs we pile on
Wet from the night
Your shoulders are strong, like mine
Your chin-line clean, warm stone
I run my fingers along the grain ...

I feel firm thigh muscles soften
Under the denim sacrament beside me
I taste the wine
In wonder at the chalice

A sip of port and gentle song
We kiss
Genuflecting fingers
Reverent and wondrous tongues
I lay my head on the dark cliffs of your chest
And feel the waves
Beating in your blood
Your arms like warm curves of land
Close around me

And deep in my body, my belly
Up rushes the sea full song
And I can only lay and let its tongues, its waves,

Break through me like surf
Like clean-cold flames
Tingling with God
Who holds my body
In his
At rest now
At rest now
The name lingers on my lips
And I
Still taste
The night
I held
The beating
Licking
Body
Of God,
And felt the blood of praise
Surge and tumble through me
The wake
Of his love

When we come through this holy awakening, or it happens within us, there is no longer any desire to go back. Any need to go back or any possibility of going back. We are on the other side of the Red Sea. We have gone through our baptism, often a baptism of blood, certainly a baptism of tears and a baptism of joy. And a baptism that takes place in our bodies, in our flesh. I don't know, maybe there are ways, but I don't know of ways to go through this baptism without it happening in our bodies.

    I think of two stories I heard of two different priests for whom this happened, when they were at prayer; one of them was actually celebrating the Eucharist and found himself aroused with a raging hard on, and felt the holiness and the bodily involvement of what he was doing in the Eucharist and in his own body. Perhaps that's another way of going through this holy awakening. Certainly the understanding or the image of having loving and erotic sex with Christ, making love to Christ, is an experience that a number of gay men have told me about, as their first deep realization that this is holy. [That] this is a way into union with the divine lover, this physical, sexual, erotic experience of spiritual and sexual joy, spiritual and sexual lovemaking as one reality.

Now, what's happening here is that we are tasting for ourselves what all the institutions talk about, what the institution of the church, what all the scripture tries to minister to us, to be a channel for us, we're tasting it ourselves. And brothers and sisters, we are tasting it outside the bounds, outside the bounds that we have been told we must not exceed: and outside those bounds, there is only sin, there's only death. Well, hey, we've been there. We've been there and we know different. Outside those bounds is life, is grace, is joy, is God, is the divine lover himself/herself. And this makes us dangerous, because we're tasting it now ourselves, we don't need in the same way the channels of grace, the structures of the church or society, because now we are tasting freedom, ourselves, in our own guts. And we are never going to be the same again. So we're dangerous people. And Hallelujah, for the danger we are to society and the church.

The downside? We see the oppression for what it is. We see the slavery for what it is, we see the cruelty and the evil for what they are. We now know what is being done to us and our brothers and sisters, in the name of God. And that is intensely painful. It's the downside. So things are moving, we're on the road, we've crossed the Red Sea, and we are really, truly free. Not totally, not totally. Those gods still pursue us because they're in us. But we are really free now. We are living a life. We are living a life. And you can perhaps see why I'm saying so strongly that this coming out, this exodus, this liberation is both within and external. Most crucially, it's within. If by some miracle of the Holy Spirit, people are actually able to remain fully in the institution (and I know some people who claim they are, and who am I to tell them what their truth is, I don't claim to do that; but I do believe if they can, it's a miracle of the Holy Spirit) they will be in the institution in a totally different way. They will not be the same person. They will not be the same member of the institution. They are now dangerous. They are now subversives. They're now spies, if you like, set out to prepare the new kingdom, the new land, the new freedom, even within the institution. So they are free, as well.

So, things are moving, there's rejoicing, but there's still the pain of leaving behind the old life and all that we knew. There's still uncertainty, there's still unknowing as to where this is going to lead us. What does this promise mean? We've come this far but we can't see all that will happen ahead of us. We're aware of the baggage we still carry. We're aware more than ever, of the bewilderment and the opposition of others. And we're aware that there are still deaths and exoduses to come. It's not over yet.

Carter Heyward talked about how when she came out publicly on radio, I think it was, or perhaps in a newspaper article, and she thought, 'I've done it now, the world knows', little realizing that every time she met someone, every time she gave a talk, every time someone else said, 'Oh you're Carter Heyward', there was the issue of 'do I come out again and again and again and again'? The exodus has to keep on being made. And it's not easy. It's never easy, especially since we've become more and more aware of just how much is against us.

So this essential movement to life begins both in a sense of emptiness and slavery, and in the awakening to new possibilities, to joy, to freedom, which shows us our slavery and promises us new life and a new way of being. This is very typical in the contemplative life, the spiritual life, and in gay and lesbian life; the parallels continue. In contemplative life, this joy very quickly gives way to aridity, to dryness in prayer, to a sense of boredom and pointlessness. We'll be talking about it more in the next session. In gay life, this joy gives way to the feeling that this is a hard road, this is not an easy road to walk. And when we realize this, when we've gotten over the dance of joy with the timbrels and the tambourines and the singing, as we come through the water of exodus, when we get over that, then we're really on the journey.

Just a word in closing about community. And I can't say this too strongly. The exodus was a community event. And in the experience of passing through the water, and then passing through the desert, it was that experience that made this group of motley people, these nomads and wanderers and slaves, it was that that made them into a people, that they experienced it together. Together! The desert monks, even though they went out into the desert alone, they very soon formed hermitages around one another to find support, to find some guidance from the older monks who'd lived the road longer. Not too many of them continued to go out and be totally alone, they found community.

Brian McNaught, a wonderful teacher and guide in this coming out process, says that until you have a community of support, don't do it. I think too of the wonderful story of the raising of Lazarus, when Jesus goes to the tomb of his friend who has been dead for days. And in spite of what everyone tells him, he orders the tomb be opened. And he stands there, calls on the Spirit of God and says to Lazarus, 'Come out'. I heard that story at the Eucharist one night when I was going through my own coming out process, and it's always been very precious to me. But the next thing he says when Lazarus comes out all bound up with the cloths of death (read, you know, what we've been bound up with in our slavery), Jesus says to the people around him, 'Unbind him and let him go free'. Lazarus needed a community to take off the binds, the bonds, the stuff that clung to him and kept him in something like death. And we as gay and lesbian people coming out need a community to do that for us. How do we really find that community? This is one of the most desperate needs, to form not just any gay community. As Joe Kramer says, 'There isn't a gay community, there's a gay population'. Amen. What we need is true community that will really be with us in this process, in this journey, take off the bonds, and lead us in a new way of being.

And here, I can't say too much about the need for people to make the journey ourselves; the need for mentors, for guides, for people who have the guts to go all the way, to go through all the exoduses, all the deaths and resurrections, all the dyings and rising to new life that we have to go through as mature, truly spiritual, gay and lesbian people.

Why is it so vital? Because very, very soon, the newly out gay person will go into the desert very quickly. We'll talk about that more in the next tape; they will very soon encounter the cost, and we have no natural community, no family, no tribe, no nation, no religious order of our own. No one's going to set up a separate country for us, although I hear some gay groups are starting to lobby for that. Well, good luck to them. I'm pleased to see they chose Hawaii as one of the main possible locations for this new country. If they get it, perhaps I'll go and become a citizen. But it's unlikely. Currently we have none, we have no natural community. At least, you know, a young black person coming out into freedom can find some sense of nurturance, some sense of solidarity with other black people also on the journey and who've gone before [them]. Too few of us have that kind of community, that kind of family to go back to, to find nurturance in, and we desperately need it.

And also we have been cut off from our sources of wisdom, we've been cut off from our spiritual heritage of the Scripture and told that it is something which condemns us. It's been used as something to bash us and kill us. So, we've been cut off from the wisdom of Scripture and the heritage of the Christian community. This is what I'm trying to recover. And we've been cut off from our gay heritage, from the heritage for example of the two spirits tradition, so called *berdache*, although that's not a word we ought to use anymore. But also the 'two spirits' of the Native American traditions, from the wisdom of gay elders and gay shamans in all kinds of traditions throughout the world, we've been cut off from them as well. And too many of our old people are caught too much in the web of trying to be what the so-called gay community tells us we ought to be, endlessly seeking youth, for example, instead of the wisdom that comes with age, which can then be offered back to us as we grow; not to condemn those people, just to recognize the sadness of what slavery does to us, and how we need to also minister to our older people and encourage them to own their wisdom and their experience.

So, there's a desperate need for gay community. We will encounter both hostility from the church who are supposed to be an agency to lead us into freedom, and from some gay people who do not want us to take this journey either, who would prefer us to remain as slaves who have sex but have it in the closet. No one ever said you can't have sex in the closet, you just can't have freedom. So I want to say that the gay person who tries to live as an open, mature, fully spiritual human being will find his or her sanity, his or her sanctity, and his or her life, as much at threat as any hermit in any Syrian desert, as any monk in any desert.

So we need each other. Discernment around coming out, around how are we being led into this Exodus: look for our points of resistance, look for the desert roads, look for the moments where we feel the need to move, where we feel the slavery chafing, where we feel the plates grinding and we feel the sense that there is more. So, let's go forward. Let's go forward with the pillar of fire of our passion, and the pillar of cloud, the sense of mystery, of possibility, of the unknown, to guide us and to encourage us. We have nothing to lose but our chains and our slavery. And what we gain is our lives.

Leave your family, your country and your father's house for the land that I will show you.

Study Guide

Discernment and courage in following God's call is the central challenge in our lives as Christians. God's call to Abraham and Sarah speaks to us as gay and lesbian people: 'Leave your homeland for the land I will show you!' We begin our journey with no map but with trust in God's promise, for always the Spirit leads us towards deeper awakening and more authentic liberation. Areas explored in this lecture include:

Christian life is always seen in the light of the death and resurrection of Jesus, and of the great stories of the People of God.

The great traditional themes of Scripture and of Christian spirituality have to take flesh in our own lives, and therefore we find our inspiration in the stories of Abraham and Sarah, of Exodus, of Jesus, of the desert monks and nuns.

God's call: 'Leave your homeland for the land I will show you!'

- The call to go out in trust with no clear maps, markers or destination
- The promise of God accompanies the call. This is our only assurance.

In the Exodus God says: 'Let my people go!' This is addressed to the gods of Egypt, to the gods of our culture, and to the gods within ourselves. We must name the slavery we have endured and even become accustomed to accept ('conscientisation').

The Call, the Promise, is always about the movement from slavery to freedom. This promise calls us to face our fear of the unknown and of the cost of freedom, and to move forward in trust.

Following God's call is at the heart of spiritual life for LGBTIQ+ people of faith. We follow in the midst of struggle, impelled forward by both the promise of freedom and the 'death' of our imagined future in the Church as we had known it.

We experience this call through Awakening on several levels. In particular:

- Discovering that our sexual desires are good and that we have a right to be fully sexual beings
- Discovering that our sexual relating can be truly holy and graced.

Awakening exposes us to the pain of the oppressive lies imposed upon us, and to the knowledge that we cannot go back to the old life, despite the security and the rewards it may seem to offer. Awakening is profoundly threatening to the status quo:

- We now see and taste and name the oppression
- We now see and taste New Life from the Source within.
- This is a journey of 'Coming Out' in society and in the church, but also, most deeply and personally, coming out within oneself. It is a continual challenge. The need to respect God's movement in relation to timing.
- Community is vital in this process:
    - We encounter the 'wilderness' very quickly
    - We have no 'natural' family or community
    - We have been cut off from our sources of wisdom
    - We will face hostility from society, church and some gay people.

The call for LGBTIQ+ mentors, elders and guides to tell their stories.

The crucial importance of ongoing discernment.

Questions for discussion and reflection

1. Consider the times in your life and loving when you have felt the pain of 'death' and the surprising joy of 'resurrection'. How has the story, the message, and the presence of Jesus inspired and encouraged you in those experiences?

2. Have you personally experienced life situations when the call to 'Leave your homeland' was urgent and seemed the only way forward? How did you respond?

3. How do you experience and understand the 'slavery' to which LGBTIQ+ people have been subjected? Is your God the God of the slaves and the outcasts, or the God of the enslavers? How would you tell the difference?

4. What are the 'gods' within you that do not want to allow your journey towards freedom to take place? How do these 'gods' maintain their influence over you?

5. What is the 'cost of freedom' for LGBTIQ+ people in our culture and in the church? What has the cost been, and what might it still be, for you personally? Is this freedom worth the cost involved?

6. Consider your own story of 'Awakening'. When did you first experience your 'forbidden' sexual desires as good? Have you ever experienced sex as holy, graced, and sacred? Have you become aware of this experience of grace among other LGBTIQ+ people? How has this changed you, your understanding of God, your relationship with the church, and your relationship with your own body?

7. What does it mean to 'come out within yourself'? How important is this? How does it relate to the various stages of coming out, and especially coming out publicly? Where are you on this journey towards full and free coming out?

8. The God of Jesus Christ always calls us to deeper freedom and fullness of life. What might this mean for LGBTIQ+ people? What might this mean for you personally—for your relationships, your career, your place in the church, your future, your sense of who you are and who you are called to be?

9. How might LGBTIQ+ Christians explore and express the communal dimensions of our faith? Have you ever experienced deep Christian community as an LGBTIQ+ person of faith? How might you personally nurture such community for yourself and others?

10. Who has mentored or inspired you as an LGBTIQ+ Christian? Who first encouraged you to begin to accept and embrace your sexuality and your spiritual call? As you look ahead, what kind of mentorship do you feel you need, and where might you look for models and inspiration as you continue to move towards justice, freedom and dignity?

4

The Desert and the Dark

Welcome to our fourth session in this series. In this session we consider the desert and the dark. One of the great things the desert teaches us is that while we are alone, we're not alone. So once again let's take a moment to be quiet together, you in your space and time and me in mine, and to recognize that we are one.

May God give us the grace to speak and to hear one or two honest words. Amen.

*

In turning to speak of the desert and the dark, I'm very specifically turning to that which really can't be spoken of. There's an old saying, that 'those who know do not speak and those who speak do not know'. So with that disclaimer, I boldly go ahead to speak. But it seems there is a need to say something that our minds can grasp, as we move deeper into the Christian life, into the spiritual life, and deeper into our experiences as gay and lesbian people.

As we were saying in our last session, Exodus and Awakening, as we come out of the sense of slavery into freedom, there's often a great sense of life and of joy, of a new juice, of a new possibility for being someone that I've always wanted to be, for having the freedom that I've always sought; I've finally arrived, I'm finally here, with tambourines and songs as in the story of Exodus. It doesn't take very long at all before we start to feel the chafe, before we start to feel, hey, it is not all so sweet out there. And even in here, there's desert territory involved in this journey. And that's what we want to talk about today.

A number of years ago, when I first left high school, I joined the Franciscan Order. As novices, we go through a beautiful ceremony called clothing, when we kneel before the priest who's in charge of the province, and say certain things, and he receives us into the order. We were wearing suits and ties, and we took off our jackets, and then he put the habit, the brown habit with the cord and the hood, over us. And it's a very beautiful moment. I remember after mass was over, there were seven of us, seven very attractive young men, all in our brown habits, and we went out into the sacristy, immediately reached for our jackets and took them with us as we went out the door. The symbol of the habit, of course, is being clothed with the new person (comes from St Paul), rather than the old person, slave to sin and all that kind of imagery. And one of the priests sort of looked at us and said, 'hmm, doesn't take long for the old man to reassert his rights, does it?' as we went out with our jackets. I mean, we just wanted to keep our jackets basically, but there's a lot of truth in that priest's observation; we can have this honeymoon period, but it doesn't take very long before we start to realize what may be involved in the journey that we've undertaken, and that can come as a rude shock. So we start to enter into a time of, I suppose, purification, of genuineness where this is not just an experience, it's a life that we're living. After the first flush of spiritual joy, we have aridity; after the coming out, we have the reality of what that means in our lives and our relationships.

I remember when I was going through this process myself of discernment around coming out very publicly in a newspaper article. And a friend of mine who's a married woman, Judy, a very beautiful woman, was helping me discern whether this was the time and the place and the way, and she said to me at one point, 'Are you prepared for the hate?' It really took me aback, knocked me over a bit. I really had to say 'no, I'm honestly not. I'm prepared for some opposition, some difficulty', but I wasn't really prepared for hate. That was one of my desert moments, it started to make me realize just what might be involved in living this life as an openly gay man. This is not a game. This is not a thrill. This is not opening night at the opera. This is a hard and long and wonderful journey that will take us into the deepest places and into the heights, if we're prepared to go with it all the way. It really is, I believe, a way to true sanctification, true holiness, true maturity as a human being, if we are prepared to let it be that for us.

There's a little quote I'd like to read from one of JD Salinger's novels (he's the guy who wrote Catcher in the Rye): 'I don't want you to go away with the impression that there's any, you know, inconveniences involved in the religious life. I mean, a lot of people don't take it up just because they think it's going to involve a certain amount of nasty application and perseverance. You know what I mean? As soon as we get out of chapel here, I hope you'll accept a little volume from me that I've always admired called God is my Hobby.' Well, the reality is that in this journey, it's not about a hobby. It's not about games. It's not about temporary excitement. It's about the day-by-day reality of living, with all its beauty, its drudgery, its boredom, its pain, its joy.

So, the desert. Why would I call this talk the Desert and the Dark? Well, first of all, because following our story of Exodus, and also the story of Jesus to a large extent, certainly the story of the desert monks in our Christian spiritual heritage, the desert is moot, it's very much the point. Exodus does not lead the chosen people, the people of Israel, through the waters into the great malls of Palestine, the great shopping centers, the entertainment centers, the Broadways of Israel, it leads them straight into a desert, and a very harsh desert at that. In the tradition, in the story, they wandered in that desert for 40 years. This was a long time. And again, in the actual story, none of the people who came out of Egypt actually ended up coming out of the desert. There's a whole generation that changed in that story. It's a long and hard road, and this is the story of Exodus. So, Israel in the desert, Christ in the desert, monks in the desert. What is the desert?

When I was a little younger, I used to take groups of students on bus tours in the Australian outback. Now, probably some of you have seen the bus tour to end all bus tours in the outback, namely the film, *Priscilla, Queen of the Desert*. Unfortunately, we didn't run into Priscilla or her kind while we were traversing the wastelands. But certainly, I got to know the beauty and the awesomeness of the Australian desert. Huge, enormous, the driest continent on Earth, the most desolate continent on Earth, apart from Antarctica. And in 13 or so trips around this vast wilderness, I got to sort of understand a bit about what the Israelites, and what the desert monks, might have experienced. I remember we pulled off the road as we would normally do in the middle of hundreds of miles of just absolute barren wasteland (with nothing between you and the west coast, north from Perth. All that desolation, all that aridity, all that emptiness, and we're in the center and there's nothing, nothing between you and the ocean). And we pulled off the road, the bus stopped and we made lunch, prepared sandwiches. I went for a little walk up the road and climbed a little mound and I looked out on this spectacular emptiness. I saw this tin canister called a bus, and these 45 or so people milling around having sandwiches and drinks and things. And it seemed to me like we were a tiny ship in an immense and hostile ocean. And the only thing that was keeping us alive was staying with that ship. If that ship were to break down, or to move out into the wasteland and not stay on this road, this dirt track, and get lost, we would die. It was that real. They call that country 'six-hour country', meaning that if you were caught there without shade and without water, you would die in six hours.

This is very hostile country. This is the desert. So, what does going out into the desert teach us? Why would a person do this? The Hebrews were led out there, the desert monks went there by choice, Christ went into the desert before he began his ministry. Why?

Firstly, the desert teaches us a great intimacy with nature. We really are exposed in very raw ways to the beauty and the grandeur and the awesomeness of nature. We also feel the artificiality of our own lives; so much of civilization, and the junk we carry around is stripped from us very readily in the desert; we start to realize just how fake it all is. Part of the reason that so much of what we carry with us from civilization appears so fake and even ridiculous when we are in the desert is that our real needs become very, very sharp and clear. You know, we often do these exercises around what are our wants and what are our needs. Well, when you're in the desert, your real needs become very clear: food, because of the experience of hunger; water because of the experience of thirst; shelter because of the experience of exposure to both intense heat and intense cold; and companionship because of the experience of loneliness. We really are reduced in the good sense to our basic humanness. And friends, there is no true spiritual life, there is no true life, without coming back, coming down to our true humanness, our natural selves, and getting rid of some of the baggage, all of the baggage.

We also become very aware in the desert of our dependency on each other, on nature to be kind to us and provide for us food and shelter, and on God, the universe, life. In this connection, we become very aware of how small we are, how fragile we are and how awesome, how beyond our control, the universe is. I'm convinced that that primal experience was what gave rise to people offering sacrifice, for example, to try to placate the gods and to get them to be kind to them, because they experienced firsthand the awesomeness, the overwhelming majesty and uncontrollability of the universe, because they lived very simply in nature.

Also in the desert, our demons are exposed. You can't play games with yourself in the desert, or if you do, very soon they'll fall apart. You get to know what your compulsions are, what your real motivations are, what your dark places are, what your fears are, what your addictions are, what your mess is. Our justifications become very clear; the way we make our lives feel worthwhile, the way we make ourselves feel important, the way we give ourselves, construct for ourselves, a sense of identity, becomes very clear in the desert. And it becomes very empty in the desert, as again, we become reduced to who we really are. So, we get stripped down to this bare essential 'me' in front of the awesomeness of what actually is. And we discover what it is we truly believe in, what it is we truly value; what it is that we've been using as gods up until now and, when they're stripped away (and the sooner the better), what we then are left with, what we then find we really believe in.

In this experience, most of the authorities that we may have looked to for definition, for codes of morality or law, or for a sense of self, are also exposed as empty and pretty worthless. And all we are left with is, what is the law in my heart? What are my true values? What do I really believe matters? Now in this, some of the heritage of the past, some of what our community may have given to us, or all of it, is put to a very severe test. And in that test, some of it may come out as being worth something. But a lot of it will come out as being worth nothing, and in fact, as being an obstruction to coming into truth, to coming into who we are and what we really believe. A friend of mine, a gay priest, who recently left a religious order in Australia, painfully had to say that he really felt the other side of it, that a lot of what was structured for him, in fact, kept him away from living a deeply spiritual life. But he had to go through a desert of loneliness and of emptiness to find that.

So, in this desert, the authorities we've looked to, including our society, including gay culture (and we'll consider that a little later), are really put to the test, and those that survive, survive, and those that don't were never worth it in the first place. This is why the desert has traditionally been seen as a place of purification, and a place of deep growth. Meister Eckhart, one of our great mystics says, 'The soul grows by a process of subtraction'. We take away the junk, and sometimes, not just the junk! Stuff that seems quite worthwhile has to go as well. We become stripped down to who we are at bottom, the absolute ground of who we are. And in this process we become open to God; we also become open to the experience of the devil, or the demons within ourselves, a very harrowing experience. It is the place of struggle.

I would like to look at the experience of Jesus when he goes into the desert before he begins his ministry, and experiences temptation; and also look at the experience of Israel, because for them, the desert is a place of regret, a place of challenge, of temptation, of betrayal, of Covenant, of becoming a people, of aimless wandering, and ultimately of the journey to the promised land. Let's keep these two paradigms in mind as we look firstly at the experience of gay people in our culture.

As I was saying earlier, after coming out, we very quickly begin to experience the cost. After the joy and delight, we have to face the fact that our jobs could be at stake, our friendships can be at stake; many people find in this experience who truly loves them for who they are, and who can't cope with this new supposed revelation ... very much our families. We all know this, the incredible traumas and struggle and pain that so many thousands of gay people go through every day, every year, in coming out to their families. So many people say I have never done anything harder in my life, mentioning the risk that is involved, and so often the rejection. I'm sure we all have close friends, if we haven't experienced it ourselves, who have been totally rejected by their families, and don't hear from them for years, if at all: tremendous pain, tremendous sense of loss and of alienation. The sense of the church rejecting us and not wanting us to be part of its life. And of course, the risk to our own lives in a very physical sense.

These dimensions of the desert strip us back, if we're open to them (and we don't take refuge in panaceas and placebos and quick answers), they strip us back to our basic selves and ask us, What really is worthwhile? What do I really believe in? What really matters? Who really are my gods? And who is with me in this journey, in this struggle, and who is not? It's a real process of hollowing out, of sifting the wheat and the chaff and finding out what really stays there. In this process, there also can be days of great regret, of thinking 'what the hell have I done?', of thinking 'I should go back', of hearing voices calling me back. Am I mad that I could think I could really live out here? We start to taste the exile, to really taste it. Before, we kind of knew it was there and were frightened of it, but now we're eating it and drinking it, we are tasting it in all its bitterness, in all its reality. The exile, the sense of being an outsider, of not belonging, of being excluded, the stigma. We feel it every time we question ourselves as to whether we should come out to someone or not, and we do that almost every time we meet someone. We experience it every time someone mentions the word gay or lesbian. And we feel something rise in us, something that both wants to cover over and protect ourselves, and something that wants to strike out and make a statement. And which do I do here? Again, we feel the chafe, we feel the rub, we feel the exile that we don't belong. We often feel it when we watch families and children; so many of us feel excluded from that. Even those of us who have had children, in gay relationships, or children from past marriages, still feel that we are in some way excluded from the fullness of family life in our society. We feel that pain when we see children and families together. This is very real, it's a day by day experience.

I said in the last tape, perhaps somewhat playfully, that not all of us live in the Castro. And even in the Castro, we feel this, so how much more in so many other cities all around the world, this constant day by day experience of exile. This is the experience of desert, of being outside of society, outside of the mainstream. Whatever jobs we may hold, however much we may go to work in suits and ties, we don't belong. We feel our dependence. Like in the desert, we feel our dependence on others. It's a painful reality. But you know, as John Boswell points out through his book about social tolerance, fundamentally we have our place in society at the mercy of the majority. Even if there are 10% of us, there are 90% of them. And they've got the structures on their side. In the place where we're filming now, there is a rainbow flag in the window. I've often thought as I've come in this place, it would just take a breath of change, just a soft breeze of change, and we would have to take that flag out because it would no longer be safe to have it in the window. I have bumper stickers on my car. So far, the windshield has not been smashed, but it could be: again, just a breath of change and it certainly would be.

This has been the reality of gay people's lives all through history. Even when we have situations such as in the Native American tribes where gay people are honored, the fact remains that that could change. Being honored and being reviled are two sides of the same coin. What's being said is these people are different, these people are special. One is saying they have a unique and gifted role and the other is saying they're scum, they're the dregs. They really are two sides of the same coin. They're saying that we are on the outside; by the rule of the majority we may be brought inside, but it remains by the will of the majority. This is not an easy thing to hear. This is not an easy thing to face. In no sense am I ever suggesting that we do not fight for our rights. In fact, this is more reason to fight for our rights, accepting this reality. At the very least, folks, it's not going to happen in our lifetime. And we know it could change, it could change; whatever rights we win can be reversed, they have been before. So experiencing this reality, that we are desert travelers, we are outside the mainstream, we do hold our rights and our freedoms to some degree dependent on the majority, feeling the rub of the exclusion, the pain of the exclusion. This is what it means to be in the desert. Being exposed to what our real gods are, this is what it means to be in the desert. Again, there is a very physical dimension to the desert and there is a very physical dimension to this. It comes down to jobs, employment, housing, fundamental rights, life itself. Again, this is not a game, this is not just a spiritual state, this is a physical fact—as the desert is a physical fact.

And also in this desert we feel the need for companionship, for support on a much, much deeper level. Think for a moment about that image of the metal canister, the bus in that vast Australian outback, that issue of survival, that outside of this canister we couldn't have survived. But part of what was happening in that canister was that people were coming together to support one another, feed one another, share with one another and journey through the desert together. And in my experiences in Latin America, I've seen people who have made an exodus from the old regimes and are going through the desert of struggle towards liberation, of building a new society against incredible odds in places such as Nicaragua and El Salvador. What they have is community, that is their gift, that is their blessing and that is what they can teach us, this need for one another, to be with one another, and to strengthen one another in this incredibly harrowing and painful and holy process of being stripped down to who I truly am. So, one of the dangers in trying to look for companionship is that we can grab for false solutions, we can look for some kind of companionship just to help us ease the pain. And that is understandable. But ultimately it's a dead end. We need to be careful of it. It's also important as we go through the desert and the dark (and there's more to come) that we remember to celebrate our liberation, and to enjoy what we have won, the freedoms we have won.

Just last night, as I was coming home to prepare this session, I'd already done a lot of work and I wanted to go over it a little more. I was faced with the choice of being with some of my gay brothers in a very sensual and supportive way or coming home and doing my work alone. And a friend said to me, 'No, you're going to be talking about liberation, Exodus, and journeying through the desert. Come out and be with us and let us support you and celebrate the liberation you're going to be talking about. You know enough about the desert to talk about it already.' So that's what I did. And I think that's precisely what we need to do as well as going through the desert; face it, accept it, live it, be stripped, but also celebrate and nurture and share the joy of the liberation we're experiencing. That is what brings us manna in the desert, brings us food in the desert and leads us through it.

So, in all of this, we experience temptations on this road through the wilderness to go back. I've had enough of this, I'm going back. I'm going to go back and get the job with the corporation, put on the suit, do the thing, pretend to be the straight guy. It's not worth it. Denial. Well, it's not so bad. It's not so bad. I mean the place I live's all right, my company's okay, my family's alright, it's not so bad. What's the problem? What's all this moaning and groaning about deserts for? It is so bad. This is classic denial. The setting up of ghettos, not that having our own space is not a good idea. We have to watch they don't become ghettos, keeping other people out and thinking we have solved the problem. Well, sorry, we haven't.

Thirdly, to despair, the temptation to despair. It's hopeless, it's worthless. There's no way forward. And this brings to mind of course all the gay suicides that we're aware of. If we're ever tempted to think it's not so bad, the desert is not so real, what's this guy going on about, just think of our gay suicides, the heritage that we carry in our blood, of how many of our gay brothers and sisters still today kill themselves, rather than face the reality of what it means to be gay in our culture. This is exile. This is the desert. This is the pain that we face. Can we walk through it together without denying it, without taking refuge in our old slavery, without finding false solutions and without despairing.

I want to look at these temptations. In the story of Jesus going into the desert, he's tempted three times by the devil in the story in the gospels, just before he begins his ministry. The first temptation in the desert is when the devil says to him, 'Turn these stones into bread.' In that temptation for us, I see the temptation for us to pretend to ourselves that the stones the church has handed us are in fact food, that the stones of self-hatred, the stones of 'it's okay to be gay but don't do anything about it'. The stones of the old code of morality in as much as it affects us, pretending that those stones actually do nourish us, that the church truly has good teaching there. It's a danger when we're feeling weak and vulnerable and lost to try to make these stones into bread. Secondly, the devil appears to Jesus and shows him all the kingdoms of the world. You'll remember our image of world from the last tape, the world as being the structures of the status quo, which keep some people down and raise a few people up at their expense. The devil says to Jesus, 'All these cities of the world can be yours, if you will fall down and worship me.' And what I like to see in that, is the temptation to materialism, to consumerism, to bowing down before the almighty dollar, whether it's pink or otherwise. It's also I believe a temptation to buy the values of the old culture in a new form, which are the values of much of the gay subculture, just in a new dress, in a new shape. It's one of the great dangers, that we get sucked into that, and in fact are bowing down before the old gods. And sure we can have all this, if that's what we want.

And the third temptation: the devil takes Jesus to the top of a high mountain and says to him, 'Throw yourself down. It's written in Scripture that the angels will support you, and you won't even dash your foot on a stone. Throw yourself down and see if God will come to your aid.' And what I see here is the temptation for us to refuse to live the ordinary, boring, painful, hard life of faith as we go through the desert. To in some sense test God, try and force God to make it all okay, to fix it all, to make it so that we don't dash our foot on a stone. Come on, you said all these things, prove it to me, instead of the hard, hidden road of faith, which is the true road through the desert, the true road through the dark, the true road into fullness of life. They are three of the temptations I believe we face as gay people, seen in the temptations of Jesus.

When we look at the experience of Israel, we see a very powerful image. It wasn't long before the Hebrews got very tired of the desert and started thinking, at least in Egypt we had meat to eat and bread to eat, we could sit around and relax a bit. And here what have we got? Nothing much. And they also started to miss the gods of Egypt, because this God was a very hidden God, a God who had no image, had no real name. And the gods of Egypt, you know, that was feasting and dancing, and at least you could focus on something. So while Moses was up on the mountain receiving the covenant, they put in all their gold and they melted it down, and they made a golden calf, a false god, a new god, a god like they had in Egypt, and set it up on a pedestal and danced around it and had a great feast. Moses comes down the mountain with the tablets of the law and is very upset and smashes the tablets. On goes the story. But the point is, this dancing around the golden calf: they're in the desert, they've come through the Exodus, they've walked a fair way into the desert, and still, they can make a golden calf. Now the golden calf was made with gold that they had plundered from the Egyptians and brought with them. So, the golden calf is actually made out of gold from the old culture, gold from the old slavery, gold from the old structures of society.

Now you might think I'm doing a number on gay subculture. Well, folks, I am. I think one of our great dangers is that we take the gold of the old culture and rework it into the golden calf, the golden calf of ageism and sexism and materialism and consumerism, mindless, absolutely mindless and heartless pleasure at the exploitation of other people. We use people, we use things, we use clothes, we use fashion, we use whatever it might be, we use ambition, we use careers, we use one another, as a god to stop the void, the pain of this hurting in the desert. And we think we've found something. But we've found less than nothing. We've found just the old stuff in a new form, just as much slavery. If we are going to accept that the journey into true gay maturity is also the journey into true spiritual maturity (and that is what I'm proposing), we have to break away from these gods both within us and outside of us, because if we don't, they will keep reasserting themselves in new forms. That is part of what has to happen in the desert, finding the false gods and disposing of them, finding more and disposing of them, being constantly purged until we can find who we truly are. Again, there's no suggestion that we don't fight for our rights, and that we don't set up enclaves where we feel safe. The danger is that we make them into the be all and end all and feel we've arrived in the promised land, when in fact, we're just in a little oasis of exile. The journey through the desert can also lead us to bitterness and enslavement if we're not open to the possibilities of joy, and the goodness of community, as I was speaking about before.

Another experience of being in the desert (and this is a very important one) is that the desert traveler can recognize other desert travelers, can be open to other poor wandering nomads who are in the desert, pushed out and rejected, and can learn the gift of hospitality, can learn the gift of solidarity, can learn the gift of being brother and sister for one another in oppression. And here I'm speaking not just of gay and lesbian people but of all oppressed peoples. It may well be that our main struggle as gay and lesbian people is for our own rights. But at the same time, we need to recognize and support and welcome and affirm all the oppressed and marginalized groups in our society. If our hearts aren't open to them, then again, we're becoming closed off into our own world. The desert teaches us justice, it teaches us compassion, because we know what it's like to be in the desert. We know what it's like to be on the margins, to be excluded, to be outside, to be one of those on whose bodies the structures are built, which give privilege to a few and enslave the many. We know that. And so we can support and struggle with all of those who are oppressed and kept down. The desert, by the way, was the place where the monks learned hospitality. You may well be aware that one of the great gifts of monasticism was hospitality, that any traveler who turned up at the door had to be welcomed as if that person were Christ. The reason was that in the desert, your very life can depend on hospitality. How much we need to learn hospitality for one another, as we struggle through this desert.

Another great experience the desert teaches us is self-knowledge. In the midst of our loneliness and our fear and our uncertainty, as this baggage of the old self is being stripped away, we learn who we really are. And this is the first principle of the spiritual life, to know ourselves. We also know what we're capable of. I'd like to read you a brief quote from Dorothy Day when she was in prison. Dorothy Day as you may well know was a wonderful woman who died not so long ago, at a good old age. She spent her whole life working for justice in places like the slums of Harlem. She was thrown into jail for picketing with militant suffragists in 1918. She writes, 'The blackness of hell was all about me. The sorrows of the world encompassed me. I was like one gone down into a pit. Hope had forsaken me. I was that mother whose child had been raped and slain. I was the mother who had borne the monster who had done it. I was even that monster, feeling in my own heart every abomination.' So in this experience, Dorothy Day learns tremendous compassion, she learns solidarity, she learns what she herself could be capable of in her own darkness. You don't get through the desert without facing our own demons. They're not all out there. They're also in here. And we have to face them as well. In fact, they're the ones we most need to face, and the ones most people are running away from at a great rate. The desert can invite us to meet them. And these, folks, are profound gifts, hard gifts, but great gifts, true gifts if we really want to grow into maturity. If we do.

So, we want to give thanks for the desert. We want to give thanks that we are treated as someone worthless and thrown away by mainstream society, because we can learn these gifts, which sooner or later everyone has to learn if they are going to grow to maturity. Because these are part of the human condition. We have the gift of starting from that place where we can most easily learn them if we are open: as I say, painful gifts, but powerful gifts.

John McNeil, a wonderful man, a wonderful priest, who was expelled from the Jesuits a few years back for his long-term work with gay and lesbian people, makes the point very powerfully that there can't be any true gay spirituality unless we do embrace this experience of exile. Because it's the truth. And you can't have a gay spirituality founded on anything but the truth. Jesus says, blessed are the poor, because it opens us to what is in us and other people. So we need to embrace it, accept it, affirm it.

One of the alternatives to embracing our exile is to react to our stigma. Now, there's been a lot of work done on what it means to be stigmatized and how different stigmatized groups react to stigma. One of the first ways is concealment. We all know that, as gay people. We can conceal it (unlike black people) if we want to. We can become militant, take up arms and become very powerful and strong and activist. Not saying that's bad, but I am saying we are still reacting from the experience of stigma. You can put down the people who stigmatize us. So we put down the straights, breeders, what would they know about how to dress? You know, 'look at that hideous shirt'. We put them down. We recognize that we're stigmatized and we try and reach up and grab the 90% and push them down, stigmatize them. The corollary to that, of course, is boosting us. Gay people have the most elegant dinner parties, gay people have the best taste, gay people are the most creative people, gay people are the most spiritual people, gay people are where it's really at. We set all the trends! Boosting ourselves to make us feel better. And again, there may be some truth in some of those things. But the thing is that we're reacting that way to make ourselves feel better. Because we're stigmatized, we're still reacting from stigma to stigma.

The fifth way of reacting is by splitting the stigmatized group. We have been put down, and now we find someone else in our group who is stigmatized, who we can put down even further and stigmatize them. Classic example: I sat at a gay pride celebration one time with a beautiful young man. And when some Leathermen came near, he reacted incredibly to these other guys ... 'Ah, look at this, isn't it sick, isn't that pathetic, god that makes me ill, I hate that'. And I sat back and thought, 'mate, they're exactly the words that straight people use about us'. Exactly the terms: sick, ill, makes me disgusted. And exactly the tone. Splitting the stigmatized group, and saying, well, you know, I'm not so bad, at least I'm not that. Now, the leather guys might have done the same thing to him because he had been a prostitute. They could easily have turned around and said, at least we weren't prostitutes. Prostitutes could turn back and say, Oh, yes, but we weren't drag queens.

The drag queens could turn around and say, well, at least we're not assimilationists. So each group is putting down the other, all reacting to stigma. Who wins in this? Not the stigmatized. If anyone wins, it's the mainstream, which is doing the stigmatizing.

And the final way of coping with stigma is to migrate, which is not totally different from concealment, the first method, and many of us have done that too, migrated in the hope of getting away from stigma. The reality of course, the bad news, is you can't; we are stigmatized. Black people are stigmatized, Jews are stigmatized. I'm not saying it's right. I'm saying it's there. What we can do is decide how we're going to cope with this. Are we going to accept the fact and face it in all its painfulness? Are we going to learn solidarity with other stigmatized groups? Are we going to learn the wonderful critique and freedom that it can offer us in relation to mainstream society? Are we going to learn the truth about human nature both within us and within other people that it can allow us to have? Are we going to learn its lessons? Or are we going to react and push it away from ourselves? 'I'm not an exile. I'm not a stigmatized person'. Again, the invitation to accept the desert.

In all of what I'm talking about, there is a kind of an encounter with death. The old self, and many of the old hopes for self, are dying. And we're facing that. We cannot be those people anymore. Not only can we not be the people that our society would have us be, but we can't be the accepted and belonging type people, the people who 'make it', that we might have hoped we could be. And that's a death. That's a very painful death. But it's the way to learn who we can be, who we are.

This is from a book by Alan Jones. 'The desert is the place of the encounter with death. It is also the place where we know ourselves to be truly free. We do not go into the desert in order to wall up our heart. We go there in order to give it away, to open it to God and to everyone.' WH Auden says, 'The garden is the only place there is, the garden is the only place there is, but you will not find it until you have looked for it everywhere and found nowhere that is not a desert.'

'To find the garden,' Jones continues, 'to give one's heart away, to be free, one must enter the desert, stop the world, face death. Now the tears begin to flow. Yet these, it is promised, are also capable of being transformed into gifts.'

If we stay with the desert, if we remain on the journey, if we don't opt for false solutions or quick, easy communities, if we don't simply react against our stigma by pushing it away, but rather enter into it as our sacred wound and learn its lessons, what happens? What happens if you stay in the desert vulnerably, openly, trustingly? What happens is that you are led into the dark. Ultimately, we will be led through the dark into another phase of life. But first, we go deeper into the dark.

All of this experience of desert and darkness that I'm going to talk about is never absolute. There are always moments of light and joy and intimacy and freedom, and we need to celebrate that as well. Okay, this is not just a neurotic pathology I'm talking about. But it is something very real and very profound, and quite painful. The dark becomes harder and harder to speak about, the more because in Western culture and in most of our Western religion we have tended to focus on the light as the image that we use. When I speak about the dark in relation to spirituality, most people don't know what on earth I'm talking about, except embracing the shadow, and that's not what I'm talking about here. In fact, it's a very traditional, ancient and mainstream theological teaching, that all our words, all our images, all our concepts, all our scripture, everything that has ever been said or imaged about God is empty. That it only just escapes being a total lie. It's a finger pointing to the moon. It's a signpost into the mystery. But the signpost is not the mystery. And the finger is not the moon. All of our words, all our images, every concept ever thought about God, everything, every word of Scripture, is just a finger or a signpost. God is the mystery. And you must leave the finger and leave the signpost to go into the mystery, into the darkness, into the absolute silence, into the nothingness of God. This is mainstream theological teaching, not heresy, not some reworking of Eastern teaching. This goes way, way back to the very earliest centuries of the church's life. Even in Exodus way back 1000s of years ago, when Moses asks to see God, God hides him in the cleft of a rock, covers him with his hand and says, 'When I pass, you may look upon my back, because no man can see my face and live.' Images of the dark, images of the inability to capture God by sight or by image or by concept. I'd like to read through a few quotes from some mystics.

'Language cannot do everything. Chalk it on the walls where the Dead Poets lie in their mausoleums,' says Adrienne Rich.

'Love winter when the plant says nothing,' says Thomas Merton.

'This word is a hidden word and comes in the darkness of the night. To enter this darkness put away all voices and sounds, all images and likenesses, for no image has ever reached into the soul's foundation, where God herself with her own being is effective,' from Meister Eckhart.

'Then alone do we know God truly, when we believe that God is far beyond all we can possibly think about God': St Thomas Aquinas.

'The ground of the soul (which for Eckhart is also the ground of God) is dark,' says Eckhart.

'I said to my soul, be still and let the dark come upon you, which shall be the darkness of God': TS Eliot. 'Yet no matter how deeply I go down into myself, my God is dark, and like a webbing made of 100 roots that drink in silence,' says Rilke, the poet.

'Nothing in all creation is so like God as stillness': Eckhart.

Again from Eckhart (perhaps the most searing of all), 'I pray God to rid me of God. For God's unconditioned being is beyond God, and all distinctions.'

And in fact, Eckhart talks about even the Father, Son and Spirit being this side of that absolute, unconditioned, void, the wasteland, the ground, the darkness, which is the Abyss as he speaks of God, where not even the distinctions of Father, Son and Spirit appear. The absolute unutterable mystery, which no eye has seen, or ear has ever heard. Jesus simply says that no man, no one has seen the Father, the absolute mystery. And in this experience of going into the dark, which the desert gives us, we are being led into the dark, into the very mystery of God. If we are prepared to be open.

And one of the reasons I'm speaking in these tapes is because too few of us know that this is the very road of Christian mysticism. This is the very heart of what it means to follow the full Christian spiritual journey, to be led through the desert, into the absolute darkness. And we'll talk about what that means in relation to God and in relation to ourselves.

How does one grow into this experience? Firstly, by following all of the gifts and the lessons that the desert has offered us, as we've talked about them. But secondly, in a very mysterious way, a very obscure way (very hard to know and very hard to speak about), we're led by a way that is very strange, and that we can't really chart or map ourselves. It too is dark. It can be very confusing, very upsetting. It shakes us up and breaks us apart, because all that we've known has to be totally transformed. We're coming into the real transformation of the human person here. Our meaning is being literally deconstructed, taken apart bit by bit. It's not just us, not just the self, which has to be totally stripped away into our absolute foundation of darkness. It's also God, God as we have conceptualized God, has to be broken apart, because that is not God. So deconstructing the desert also has to be applied, has to do its work, on God.

St John of the Cross, one of the greatest mystics of all time, in probably the classic formulation of this way, says, and I'll read this in full: 'To come to what you do not know, you must go by a way you do not know. To come to what you do not enjoy, you must go through where you do not enjoy. To come to what you do not possess, you must go through where you do not possess. To come to what you are not, you must go through where you are not. If you wish to be all, wish to be nothing in anything. If you wish to know all, wish to know nothing of anything. If you wish to enjoy all, wish to possess nothing of anything, nothing, nothing, nothing. And even on the mountain, nothing.'

DH Lawrence says it perhaps a little more easily for us, although no less searingly: 'Are you willing to be sponged out, erased, canceled, made nothing? Are you willing to be made nothing, dipped into oblivion? If not, you will never really change.' Because the self that I have known, if I'm going to really change, that self has to break apart, has to become nothing. So that the true ground, the true self, the true who I am, the true name that I have in the mystery of God, which I don't know, which no mouth has ever spoken, or could speak, that true name, can only be found underneath, beyond, deeper than, all the names and words and sounds and images. And the way to that, is through them all, as they all fall away, become empty, become dust and ashes in our mouth. This is not an easy path. This is the deeper part of the desert.

You note that I was saying this has to happen as well to God, as we have understood that God, to the God of our fathers, to the God of our church, and that's the most painful part of all. Simone Weil, who was a wonderful Jewish Christian mystic earlier this century said, 'There are two atheisms of which one is a purification of the notion of God.' But folks, it's experienced as an atheism, it's experienced often in the spirit, in the soul, in the bone, as if I no longer believe in

God. This is what is happening to the mind. It's all falling apart. It's falling away. And we don't know what is happening to us, the more so because we felt we were being faithful and walking on the road as faithfully as we could, learning the lessons of the desert, accepting our exile, becoming nothing, having the old gods and structures stripped away and becoming mature gay and lesbian people. And now we're thrust into this darkness and what the hell has happened? And that, again, is why I speak, that is why John of the Cross wrote to say, 'This is what may be happening, have a look'.

Of course, this doesn't happen all at once. For some people, there are defining moments where they can say it's begun. I can remember myself for a moment, after a very profound experience where I really felt my life was on the line, in jeopardy, my sanity, my spirituality, and I felt that God had absolutely betrayed me, had led me into this trick, had betrayed me. And I came through that and found trust again. And it was after that, that suddenly God disappeared. And all that was left was absolute absence. I was still teaching at that point, and I remember teaching a religious education class to 18-year-olds. When someone spoke the word God, it was as if my whole guts looked up and said, Where, where? As if I was looking out the window on the road for God. This experience of absolute absence, when it begins to fall away, and the message of people like John of the Cross is, 'Yes, this is what has to happen. Stay with this. Stay with this. Don't run, don't run from it'.

Of course this goes contrary to what most people expect about what spiritual life should be like. Yeah, it should be more and more light, more and more joy, more and more feeling together, feeling integrated, feeling good about myself. It's the opposite of what we tend to expect. And that expectation adds to our sense of confusion, lostness and loneliness; we don't feel as if other people can understand us. It also goes contrary to a lot of what new age teaching tends to be saying, not all of it, but some of it. And to that extent, I'd say it's definitely missing the boat. It's also something that not many people inside or outside the church really want. And frankly, who can blame them? It is, however, the holy road, the holy road of purification.

It's not always felt like that. It felt very bewildering and frightening at times. And yet there is often a deep sense of assurance. This is the only way forward, through this, not around it, not past it. So, I want you to listen to these words as a gay or lesbian person. All our old structures fall apart, society, family, church, our sense of self, who we thought we were, our morality, our moral code, what we thought was right and wrong begins to fall apart. Religious rituals become empty, become meaningless, often routine, painful to experience. We feel as if we're an outsider, we feel as if we're excluded from them. We see our own compulsions, our own weakness, our own hypocrisy, we feel our need, our powerlessness, our dependency on others, and we feel as if we're losing control of ourselves in our life. Religious language and God language become empty and meaningless, empty, empty, seem to say almost nothing if they say anything at all. God seems to disappear, certainly the God we have known disappears, and we can't find any sense of that God being with us in this experience of being gay and lesbian. It's a sense that we've been betrayed by this God, the God we learned as a child, perhaps the God we loved for many years. A deep sense of loss, almost despair around losing this God. We feel like we've been taken out of life, as if we no longer belong, as if our life is in some ways over. There's no future for me. It's finished. We might as well close up shop, and maybe start the whole thing again. It's hopeless, emptiness, meaninglessness, aimlessness, almost despair. And yet, one continues on. Thomas Merton made a comment about why we continue on in the midst of this; he said, 'you know, in some ways, contemplatives can't help themselves, they just can't help themselves'. And I feel a bit that way about gay and lesbian people who stay on the road in spite of all this. It's like we can't help ourselves. What else is there to do? I keep walking, I keep walking. In all of this, the new person is, thank

God, being formed, in the darkness, far beyond our control or our conceptualization. TS Eliot says, 'I will wait. I will say to my soul, wait, wait without hope. Because hope would be hope for the wrong thing.' Anything we conceptualize or hang on to, is not it. So we have to let go and hang on to nothing, and just be in the dark. The Holy Spirit is taking over and is leading us in ways we could never imagine. John of the Cross says, 'If you want to go to where you are not, you must go by a way in which you are not.' The Holy Spirit is doing it in us. We can't do it. We can't travel this terrain, this darkness of desert ourselves, we can't. If we can become receptive and passive in a good sense, the Holy Spirit will lead us in ways we will never understand.

I asked you a few moments ago to listen to those points that I enumerated, which are characteristics of the darkness. As a gay and lesbian person, I guarantee you that if you are truly on the journey, as a religious or spiritual person or in some sense a Christian gay and lesbian person, you have tasted those experiences. You've tasted the old structures falling apart, rituals becoming empty, a sense of powerlessness, finding our compulsions, our addictions, a sense of losing control, the emptiness of religious language and God language, the God you've known disappearing. You've felt as if you've been taken out of life, your life is over, it's meaningless, it's empty, it's aimless, as if the whole thing's hopeless, but you've got to keep walking anyway. You've tasted all this, it's already happening in you. This is what I'm saying. This is a path into the dark. This is a path into transformation, if we can walk it vulnerably and openly and with integrity and trust in the God of the darkness, the God we can't see, the God beyond names, who is calling us into this darkness, and is with us in the darkness. In fact, not just with us, *is* the very darkness itself. The God who is all that we are, the very ground of our being.

Now, I'm not saying that all gay and lesbian people who are on the track have reached this depth of spiritual maturity. I am saying this is a path. This is a true way into this level of depth, this level of spiritual maturity. Gay and lesbian experience is not something to be shunned, nor is the depth of Christian spirituality. You might note that in the first talk of this series, I said that one of the most important principles of the spiritual life is that our spiritual and historical lives are not separate. John of the Cross wrote some of his most wonderful poetry around dark night, around experiencing the God within the darkness, in prison, in torture in Toledo. These things are not separate; what happens in our spirit and what happens in our external historical lives are enmeshed and feed each other. Similarly, our gay and lesbian experiences feed and lead us into these deeper places, if we're open to them.

I'd like to say a word now about AIDS. I think that AIDS has become a very powerful and profound road into deep and true spirituality, through all its pain, through all its agony, through its loss and grief and despair. We hear more and more people talking about the sense of expansion that they feel at the deathbeds of friends. We see incredibly heroic commitment to other people, with no reward, with nothing to take away from it, except the experience of being with that person in their pain and in their suffering and in their death, in their dying. Matthew Fox says, 'It's one thing to be empty. It is an even deeper thing to be emptied.' Pain does this. It empties us if we allow it to. This emptiness is what we're coming to through this darkness. And AIDS is one of the great, I hesitate to say, gifts. I don't believe that in one sense. I mean, these things are tragedies, they are great catastrophes; the crucifixion was a great catastrophe, a great tragedy. The deaths of tens of thousands of gay men throughout this country, and many hundreds of thousands of people throughout the world through AIDS is a great tragedy. But it can become a pathway into this kind of emptiness, darkness, vulnerability and trust. And it's quite clear that it is becoming that for very many people, as we see an extraordinary amount of spirituality, of deep spirituality, hearts opening all over the place, of people who care for people as they die, of people who die as they die themselves. Again, not everyone, but it can be a true pathway, one of the great messages, one of the great learnings for our culture and our church in this time. Thank God, there are a few people, Bishop Thomas Gumbleton for example, who say that the church has to become humble enough, and to learn from us in this experience of AIDS, about what it means to be emptied, and what it means to come to true loving. And he asks us, 'Can we be patient enough with the church to teach the church?' That's quite a tall order to ask us. The very fact that you and I are sitting here with these thoughts says that in some way, our experience of being gay and lesbian has led us on the path, otherwise we wouldn't be here. And we certainly wouldn't still be listening. I think we would have walked away from this stuff a long time ago, saying this guy's full of shit. Maybe I am. Those of you who are still here, I think, know that there's something true in what I'm saying. We've had to go through a lot of pain and darkness, we've had to lose our sense of self, we've had to lose a lot of our sense of who God is, a lot of our sense of morality, most of our sense of morality, a lot of our sense of direction, to find something not based so much on words or concepts or rules or rituals or doctrines. We've been deconstructing the god we've been given, or rather allowing that god to be deconstructed for us, because it's the Holy Spirit who's doing this, and finding our deeper inner sense. At its very best, this deep inner sense is that true law which is written on the heart in love by the Holy Spirit. It's the ground of the soul. It's the god beyond god. It's our true name, and our deepest place.

I'd like to read a very brief poem that Alan Jones quotes, written by a friend, an anonymous woman, about this process.

> I will show you the skins I have shed, left in the grass as I crept away, they are proof that I have lived.
> Skin one, docile child
> Skin two, obedient adolescent
> Skin three, scholar masked in niceness
> Skin four, stunning career girl

Skin five, charming child
Skin six, loving wife
Skin seven, marvelous mother
Skin eight, admirable Christian
Skin nine, heroic savior of abandoned children
Skin ten, nervous breakdown, entering the dark, skinned alive.

That's the process we're talking about. In fact, this shedding of the skins was one of the ancient images of going up into the dark mountain of God. Moses taking off his shoes was seen as shedding the skins of the old selves, the old identities, which have to be deconstructed over and over again, until we (after the nervous breakdown, after our coming out, after our losing all we ever thought we had or thought we were), are skinned alive. Of course, we have all made compromises, and we make them all the time. We're not perfect, it's an ongoing road. But we've had to consciously be with it, with our inner truth, and that's our gift.

These compromises we've made, they can be undone. The fact that we're trying to go with that inner truth, trying to be on the path, is the far more crucial thing. If we can allow ourselves to do this, over and over again, we can be led by this hidden sense of knowing, this knowing in unknowing. The ancient mystics referred to this darkness as 'light which is so brilliant it blinds us'. What is happening is our spirit is being flooded with the uncreated light of the divine itself. And this is so overpowering, we experience it as total darkness, as blindness, as that which undoes everything. But in fact, it's the communication of the very life of God. So this inner eye of love will lead us, on and on and on.

How much I want to say to gay Christians, particularly young gay Christians, 'Don't leave, don't leave the Christian way. You don't need to. Go into the desert, go into the dark, come out, let yourself be led into the desert and into the dark. And it will teach you everything'.

I want to say something brief about sex as a teacher; this is especially true for gay men, not only for gay men, but particularly for gay men. You don't get through the dark without the most profound receptivity, the most profound emptiness and opening of all that we are, every layer of being, every single layer of being has to be totally opened, totally receptive, in a sense passive, to allow the action of God in the darkness to be done to us, in us, with us. Now this receptivity and passivity is often characterized as feminine, rightly or wrongly, and gay men get most of our shit from the culture because of our receptivity, our passivity in sex. But folks, this is the very thing we need to learn. The very thing we need to learn, particularly as men. There's the openness and the receiving of the divine, the passivity to the divine, which we as gay men need to learn. And this also, I believe, needs to be physical. And here is something we can teach other men on the journey of spirituality, what it means to be receptive and open and vulnerable and passive to the divine lover. Sex can teach us this in a very special and unique way.

Sex I think, by following our desires, our fantasies, our needs, our compulsions and our joys, breaks down the old barriers, the old values, the old securities, the old senses of self, it breaks down the old morality. We discover who we are, what's really in there in the dark, we discover the dangers within ourselves, we discover what we could be capable of, and we make friends with it: or if not friends, at least we make some kind of alliance where we keep it in balance. We gradually come to be at home with all of this, of who we are, at peace. 'This is me, all of this stuff, the good, the bad, the dangerous, the not so good, the beautiful'. The issue is that we don't become snared by any of it, we keep moving; the desert nomads kept moving. We continue on the journey, we don't become caught in any of the stuff. But honestly, what can teach us about this stuff the way sex can; it's so available, it's so there, it's what we want to do anyway. If we're open to it, it can really teach us. We have to find inner balance, not through rules and commandments that someone gives us, but in our own bodies, in our own flesh, in our own gutsy, earthy desires, not just in some interior spiritual world. This balance is really at the heart of spirituality, coming to a balance, where nothing is denied, everything is accepted, everything is held, everything is let go.

Merton says, 'accepting everything, rejecting nothing, everything is emptiness, everything is compassion': being in that place and just holding it all, openly and vulnerably and trustingly. So let sex teach us where it can. Again, it's risky, there will be mistakes, we will have dead ends, we'll get stuck. But is that a reason not to make the journey?

So, we've gone through a lot. Where does all this lead us? What happens is that gradually, almost without our realizing it, what happens within us is a deeper and deeper surrender. A deeper and deeper letting go on ever deeper levels of our being, of everything. It's an active surrender. This is not abrogation of responsibilities or anything like that, although that may be called for too sometimes. But it is just a profound and graceful opening up. Absolute surrender, we don't need to cling to anything anymore. We just hold it silently, trustingly in the dark and in the stillness, the still center surrounded by silence, as Dag Hammarskjold calls it. We begin to discover almost to our quiet surprise that where before there was pain, now there is peace. Nothing dramatic, just quiet peace. The letting-go, the losing-control, that thing that we've been frightened of so much in our lives and especially in sex that everyone's running from, losing control. Now we let go of it, we surrender control, we hand it over more and more gracefully. We accept the not knowing.

One of the great ancient mystical treatises says, 'The more you ascend, the less you understand, because the cloud is dark that lit up the night.' This is not some easy knowing, this is a knowing in unknowing, a knowing you can't cling to and hold as 'my possession'. It's a knowing in silence, a knowing beyond knowing, a certain kind of chaos, unpredictability: we let it go, we accept it as part of the human condition. This is what is asked, this is what is given. And this is fundamentally inarticulable. There are no words about this state, or for this state. One beautiful attempt to say something about it by a monk from Camaldoli down at Big Sur: 'Faith when it is authentic takes me beyond security into a realm where peace may indeed be found, but only in an unmoored drifting into the vast sea of reality.' And he gives this beautiful line: 'I cast the anchor of my life down, and I let its line run deep into the unfathomable God on whose bosom I float. Two certitudes reassure me: the one, it is not madness to be adrift on this sea; the other, I am not alone on this sea.'

In this inarticulable moment, we also need models. I think of Oscar Romero, the wonderful Archbishop in El Salvador. He literally stands at the crossroads, having seen his priests murdered, his churches desecrated, himself abused and battered, and one of his priests tortured to death. And he's made the journey from being the good company man who was the safe Archbishop to being utterly empty. He stands at the crossroads, dirty and battered, and says, 'I can't. You must. I'm yours. Show me the way.' And from that moment, he's then led into the crucifixion, into the utter surrender of self. And he says then, of course, 'I will rise again in the people of El Salvador,' which he does, that's always the promise. And it's at this moment, it's in this darkness, this utter surrender, which can look like despair and yet isn't despair, when we're clinging to nothing, no security, that we have the deepest encounter with God. Dag Hammarskjold says, 'The night in Gethsemane when the last friends left you, have fallen asleep, all the others are seeking your downfall. And God is silent. As the marriage is consummated.' This is when the covenant is made, when the people of Israel in the desert become the people of God. In this dark desert, we become the people of God. Let's not run from this desert.

Gradually, very simply, one comes to be at home. Very simple, no fireworks, very simple, at home. The center begins to emerge, who we truly are. A quiet sense of unity, a gentle light, a place gently to stand, fragile and weak, but unmistakably there. We come totally empty.

Eckhart says that whenever God finds someone, finds anything, totally empty, God can do nothing but pour herself /himself utterly and fully into that creature. Because God cannot allow anything or anyone to be totally empty'. So, our emptiness brings to us the full outpouring of God, God's self into our deepest spirit.

How can I say how this is for a gay man, for a lesbian woman? I don't know. In one sense I can, in one sense I can't. At this place, everything is one. It's not an issue of how do I integrate my gay life with my spiritual life, there is only one life. There's only one ground in our being, there's only one emptiness, one capacity for God. And as a gay man, it's a gay capacity for God. Into that capacity, into that emptiness, God will pour himself, herself.

Things to watch out for, just in closing, as we journey through this desert, in this darkness, thinking we've arrived prematurely. Watch it. We could be clinging to something, saying ah! I've arrived. Despair and neurosis. Neurosis is real, it needs to be dealt with, deal with it. Getting stuck circling around the same spot; sometimes we need a mentor and a guide to help us with that. Bitterness and cynicism: this is hard stuff, bitterness and cynicism are real temptations, particularly as we grow older I think. Grasping for placebos and lollipops, something to make me feel better. Doesn't do too much harm if you don't cling too tightly, but we need to watch it. Overdramatizing: oh my god, you know, it's so terrible, it's so awful, I feel so depressed, it's so dark. Let's just be simple.

On the other hand, we can trivialize our darkness, we can trivialize our pain, 'oh it's not so bad'. 'What are they complaining about'? It is bad, it is painful, it is exile, it is darkness, it is death. In fact, one of the main modern spiritual writers Ruth Burrows says that at this point, it is not too strong a word to say annihilation of the self, of the ego self—not the deep self—but annihilation. I mean, this is the journey, the death to self, which all the traditions speak of. Beware of wallowing in misery. Beware of not listening to our own doubts and our own self questioning. And being aware of listening to them too much.

Helps: an honest and insightful spiritual companion, someone to talk with and share with, particularly someone who's been on the road a little longer. A healthy sense of humor. Ordinary common sense, and common ordinary releases and enjoyments: absolutely crucial. Go into a hot tub, for God's sake, have a bottle of wine. I mean, skip meditation and prayer and go and see a movie occasionally. Don't do it all the time. An appreciation of the simple. This process is not a process of evermore complex and esoteric spirituality. Absolutely the opposite. It's a process of utter simplification. Leonard Bernstein says in his mass, or Stephen Schwartz, he wrote the lyrics: 'God is the simplest of all'. Blessed simplicity, that's the touchstone, and patience. Being prepared to wait and wait and wait again.

So, as John of the Cross said, 'Oh night that guided me more surely than the dawn, night that has united the lover with the beloved.' And again, 'By night we shall go, by night, to seek the fount of living water, only our thirst for our guide, only our thirst for our guide.' Blessings on the journey.

Study Guide

As we move ahead on our journey of spiritual and sexual integration and liberation, and if we are open enough, we soon begin to experience the reality of exile, rejection, stigma, and radical vulnerability. The 'desert' or the 'wilderness' is a place of growth, purification, testing and searing self-knowledge. If we remain faithful, our old ideas of God and of goodness will be hollowed out and broken apart. 'God' may seem to disappear. We know only a painful sense of failure, absence and emptiness. Over time we may come to find ourselves at home in the 'darkness' and the 'unknowing'.

Part One: The Desert

After the new joy and freedom of Exodus and Awakening we very soon enter the 'Desert', where we begin to taste the reality of exile, rejection, and vulnerability in the midst of our concrete, daily life.

The 'Desert' can be a place of growth, purification, testing and self-knowledge. We see this in the story of God's people wandering in the wilderness, in the temptations faced by Jesus in the desert, and in the experience of the desert monks. Why is the actual experience of the desert, and the desert as spiritual metaphor, so important?

- Immediate and intense intimacy with nature
- Our basic human needs become sharp, clear, and unavoidable
- We discover our fragility, our interdependence, our vulnerability
- We encounter our own inner 'demons'—the deep inner motivations and fears that we have never truly faced
- We encounter the awesome beauty and vastness of the universe, and our place within it
- We are inevitably 'stripped' and begin to discover our true values and beliefs.

The 'temptations of Jesus' for LGBTIQ+ Christians:

- To believe that the messages of Church and society must be 'bread' for us, and if they are not then it is our fault
- To bow before the gods of the culture—whether mainstream or queer
- To reject the ordinary, daily, hidden life of faith, hope and love.

The 'temptations of the People of Israel' for LGBTIQ+Christians:

- To despair, to want to go back to the safety and comfort of the 'closet'
- To dance around the 'golden calf' of gay/queer subculture.
- The issue of stigma: the ways stigmatised people cope:
    - Concealment
    - Militancy
    - Denigrating mainstream society
    - Boosting ourselves as a stigmatised group
    - Splitting our own community
    - Migration.

The alternative: to accept the reality of exile, to embrace the desert experience and learn its lessons of self-knowledge, justice, solidarity with other exiled people, and freedom from the gods of the culture; to become open to discovering a whole new way of being. We encounter life, love, ourselves, and God, beyond the structures, dictates and expectations of society and church—here, in the desert.

Part Two: The Dark

If we walk the desert roads with fidelity and trust, we are led even deeper—into the Dark.

God, and deep encounter/union with God, are beyond all words, feelings, and concepts.

Growth towards this encounter/union is deeply 'dark', often painful and confusing. Our most foundational structures of meaning, of 'self', and of God are gradually, sometimes ruthlessly, deconstructed. Tentatively, over time, our 'true self' may begin to emerge.

'There are two atheisms, of which one of a purification of the notion of God'.

This inner growth seems contrary to what many of us expect. We feel radically disoriented as we are emptied of our reliance on structures of society, church, family, career, morality, sense of purpose, and sense of self.

Religious rituals, symbols, and languages become empty and meaningless. This is often profoundly painful. We feel we are going backwards.

We see our own weakness, compulsions, powerlessness. We feel as if we are losing control of our life.

'God' disappears—we know only a sense of dark and painful absence.

We feel excluded from life, as if life is over for us, and everything becomes pervaded by a sense of meaninglessness and hopelessness.

Despite all this, something in us continues on, seemingly blind and without purpose or direction, yet somehow sensing that this is the only way forward.

In all of this, through God's hidden and silent initiative, the true self is gradually emerging.

Many LGBTIQ+ people experience a very similar process because of the call to embrace our sexuality fully and freely. Living the truth of who we are with depth, reflection, and integrity can become a clear way into this level of profound spiritual growth.

Sex as teacher: being honest and reflective as we explore our sexuality can foster self-knowledge, unravel old structures, nurture receptivity and active passivity, confront us with the edge of losing control, and lead us towards self-acceptance and inner balance.

This journey leads to profound surrender and utter trust, as we let go of our lives, come to be at home in the dark and the not-knowing, and as our deep, hidden, inner centre gradually begins to draw our entire being towards wholeness.

Questions for discussion and reflection

1. Consider your own 'desert' experiences as you have moved towards fully accepting yourself as an LGBTIQ+ person. How has it been for you? Think of one important story or experience of 'exile' in your life as an LGBTIQ+ person of faith. How did you handle this? What did you learn from it? How did it change you? Would you do anything differently now?

2. 'Learning to embrace the exile'. What does this mean to you? How do you react to this idea? Is it possible? Is is necessary? What are the potential gifts and lessons, and also the potential pitfalls, of this kind of approach to experiencing 'exile'?

3. How have you experienced, and how have you reacted to, the stigma that is often imposed on LGBTIQ+ people? Consider your inner feelings, but also your actions. How do you deal with stigma? How have you seen other LGBTIQ+ people deal with it? What has inspired you? What has concerned you?

4. Have you ever experienced the unique gifts that can come from being on the margins—in society as a whole, and also in your family,

community and church? Have you been able to embrace these gifts? Have you seen others doing this, and what have you learned from them?

5. Who has offered you 'hospitality in the desert'? Who has given you support, encouragement, and strength as you have struggled with times of feeling excluded, rejected, or condemned? Have you offered this kind of hospitality to other LGBTIQ+ people?

6. In what areas of your life do you find yourself still trying to 'fit in', to be invisible, or to 'pass'? What motivates you to do this—not just on a practical level, but more deeply, in your heart and soul?

7. What are some of the 'old skins', the old self-identities you have left behind? Did you let go of them readily and gracefully, or was it a real struggle? Has it been worth it? What 'skins' or 'identities' still remain that you may be called to let go of? How do you feel about this kind of ongoing stripping and surrender?

8. How has your journey through the desert and the darkness affected your relationship with God, and with the church, and how has it changed your understanding of the spiritual life?

9. What have your sexual desires, experiences, fantasies and joys taught you about yourself? Are there still areas within you where you are reluctant to look? Could the Holy Spirit be gently calling you to explore those areas?

10. Consider one of the darkest times or experiences of your life. How has it changed you? How did life look to you before and after undergoing this experience? How has it changed your understanding of God?

11. How have your images, ideas and concepts of God changed over the years? Have you ever experienced emptiness, dryness and a sense of

pointlessness in your prayer and your spiritual life? How did you respond in those times, and how have you moved forward, over time?

12. Do LGBTIQ+ Christians have any real ways of avoiding this deep journey through the desert and the dark? What would they look like? How have you avoided this journey? How have you embraced it? Where have you found the hope and trust to keep walking along this road of emptiness and unknowing?

5

Liberation

Welcome to the fifth session in our series. In this session we'll be considering liberation, and the communion of love, the land, the experience beyond the desert and the dark. And as we begin to speak and to reflect about this wonderful mystery, let's take a moment of quiet, a moment of silence, to just allow our hearts to be open, to be in reflection, to be in wonder before the mystery that we'll be thinking, speaking and wondering about.

*

And so we call on all our gay and lesbian saints, on our brothers and sisters who have gone before us into liberation and communion, to be with us, to give us their love and their guidance in our speaking, in our listening, in our loving, and in our learning, in our living, and in our dying, through Christ our Lord, Amen.

*

Let me take a moment to read you a quote from Thomas Merton that perhaps sets the scene for this fifth session, and also recaps some of what we considered in our last session, the Desert and the Dark. Merton says, 'The death by which we enter into life is not an escape from reality but a complete gift of ourselves, which involves a total commitment to reality. For when Jesus said the kingdom was to be won by violence, he meant that it could only be bought at the price of certain risks. And sooner or later, if we follow Christ, we have to risk everything in order to gain everything.'

So let's consider some of those thoughts of Merton's, as we move from the land of the desert, the land of the darkness, towards the land of liberation, the experience of freedom. This involves a total gift of who we are, a total gift of ourselves. This has to be not just the false self but the true self that we've come to know, even in just a small way, through the darkness. It involves a commitment to reality. You know, often a spiritual life, particularly contemplative life, is seen as an escape: people running away to the convent or the monastery or the desert, escaping reality. And Merton is saying, No, it's nothing like that at all. In fact, it's a total commitment of the whole person who has become liberated, who's becoming free, who's becoming themselves. It's a commitment of that person to reality, to the truth of the human condition, to the truth of who we are, to the truth of our situation in the world and of what it asks of us. It also involves great risks. The spiritual life is not a cocoon where we can just be safe from any danger. Quite the opposite. The spiritual life is the risk of all that we are, of our whole life itself. And very often in living the spiritual life, we feel that our very life is on the line. And it truly is. It's also a place of hope, a hope that is, in some ways, unable to be grasped or even expressed. But it's hope that keeps us alive, keeps us going through the night. And it's the hope, fundamentally, in the coming of the kingdom, in the coming of the reign of God. And we'll talk a little bit about this later on. Because the kingdom, the reign of justice and peace is absolutely at the heart of all true human maturity, gay, lesbian or otherwise. And it's certainly at the heart of all Christian spirituality. This is not just a private, personal journey. This is a journey with profound implications for the whole of the world, for the whole of creation. It's not just my own liberation that is at stake.

I'd like to refer for a moment to the spiral nature of the spiritual life. Probably as we spoke about exodus and awakening, as we spoke about the desert and the darkness, and now as we speak about liberation, there are things which will strike a chord inside you, and you'll say, Yes, I know something of that. This is because the spiritual life is probably best imaged as a spiral, which begins and spirals down in ever decreasing circles until it finally becomes one. And as you spiral around, you are in fact going deeper, but you're also returning to the same place. If this side of the spiral, for example, were the darkness, this side were the light, you would be touching that place, but at ever deeper levels. So whatever level we're on, when we hear the language of light and liberation, and when we hear the language of darkness and struggle, and pain and death, we can relate to it because we all have some of those experiences in our lives. But it doesn't necessarily mean we are at the deepest level of darkness, or at the deepest level of light; there are always more profound levels of liberation, more profound levels of letting go. At the same time it is linear, we are going deeper all the time. And there are phases in that.

So there is a period when everything becomes one, when the darkness of the night of the soul, the darkness of spirituality, the darkness of activism, the dark night of action, when all that we do, all our work in the world, or our work for justice, for example, becomes empty and full of ashes, and seemingly hopeless. And there are times when there's a dark night of sex, when our sexual loving, our sexual relating becomes empty too. And when there is a sense that we need to go somehow deeper even than sex, deeper even than prayer. And this is when all these different phases of who we are, are becoming one, and going into a very deep part of the spiral, where we're seeking something that can't be grasped, that in a sense almost can't be experienced. And so you find people who have a lot of sex, people who have a lot of action, people who have a lot of contemplation, all saying the same thing as the spiral goes down, which is that somehow there has to be something more, something deeper. And this is when we really enter into the dark night, into the desert, into the darkness.

All of this is really to say that we are becoming whole, that all these facets of our lives are really facets of the one person. And the call to wholeness, to liberation, is to me, to who I totally am, not just to my prayer life, not just to my action, not just to my sex. It's to all that I am.

As we go on, two questions become very critical. One is, why are we on this journey in the first place? What is the purpose of this? What's the point of all this, especially when it becomes intensely painful? Why bother? You know, there's a saying in Buddhism, better not to start the journey at all, but if you do, better to finish. But better not to start; there's so much pain and struggle involved. And the other question is, once we have gone on the journey, what will sustain us? What keeps us going? What is our hope? What is the hope to which we're called? For a Christian, this always has to be seen in terms of the death and resurrection of Jesus. The death and resurrection of Christ is the central myth, the central paradigm of all Christian living, all Christian loving. We have to go through the death, there is no other way. And that is good news. Doesn't always feel like it, but it is the heart of the good news. This is an utter and complete surrender of everything, of all we thought we were and could be, into the love of God. For what? For what? What's the point of it? It's for the building of the reign of God, it's for the building of justice, peace and freedom, in my own life, in my own heart, and in all the world, not just for me. So this journey through darkness, through death, is profoundly political as well as personal.

One of the great issues and questions of spiritual life is whether it is something that becomes so private it has no implications in the political life of the world at all. And there are certain parts of our church that would much prefer to see us remain non-political. The fact of the matter is that someone who goes deeply into the dark night and who is becoming alive to the reign of God within their own body, within their own spirit, in who they are, is someone who is a profoundly political person in the sense that they are becoming free and therefore dangerous. Therefore all their actions, everything they do and are, all their relating is about building justice and love and freedom. It has nothing to do with the values of the world as we discussed in our third session, nothing to do with the values of the gods of our culture. An utterly free person! We think of Jesus, for example, who died in a very literal sense, but his death was profoundly political, profoundly liberating. We think of Latin America, where more and more a religion that was very much in the sacristy has become an incredible force for change; so much so that governments like Nicaragua, for example, are collaborating with conservative elements in the church to keep down this community movement of liberation that comes from the Gospel. We think of people like Oscar Romero, for example, a profoundly political person, because he himself became liberated in the spirit of the gospel. We even think of a mystic like John of the Cross, whose liberation, whose journey into truth, involved him becoming imprisoned for months and tortured and flogged and starved. This is not just a private journey that we're on. In many ways, whether it's political or personal, it will feel like we're dying. Often, it's obvious when people are, for example, being tortured in Latin America; it's not always so obvious when we're struggling for justice in the political climate of the United States, when we're, for example, going to the United Nations, as two gay men did in Tasmania in the country that I come from. It's not as obvious sometimes when we're sitting at our prayer, when we're going through our own sexual freedom and liberation. But often it does feel like we're dying. How else could it feel? The liberation is not always immediate, it's hard won. So, all of this is to say there is no dichotomy between true spirituality and true action; true action does not come from our own compulsions or our own ego, but comes from who we truly are and are called to be.

This talk of building the kingdom, it's a very complex and subtle reality. I mentioned Nicaragua. I have a number of close friends in Nicaragua, both Nicaraguan and from the United States. I remember sitting one night with one of these people in Berkeley, over dinner discussing the situation in Nicaragua, which had become worse and worse, and is still becoming worse and worse, and discussing what it means to struggle for the kingdom, what it means to believe that there could be liberation. And I tell the story also, for us who are in any way gay activists, involved in the struggle for gay liberation, whether simply in our own bodies or in the world at large. I said to my friend Elena, 'You know, it's not going to happen. It's really not going to happen. We've been struggling for the kingdom of justice and peace for 2000 years, in one community after another after another. And now we're struggling in Nicaragua. And we're struggling in the United States, and we're struggling in Tasmania, and we're struggling in all these countries around the world for gay liberation. In some true sense, it's not going to happen. And if it happens in this community, it'll be fragile, and it may well fall apart. And if it doesn't, there will be other communities where we still have to struggle. Our whole lives go into this. In Nicaragua, they say, maybe our struggle will bear fruit in 200 years' time, in our great grandchildren's time. We hope it does, we can only give our lives for the struggle'. So I said to her, 'in a sense it's not going to happen. And in another sense, it's already happened. Because look at people like you (this beautiful incredible woman sitting across from me), look at people like Raphael who's a leader in the older peace community in Nicaragua, look at women like Ersacillia from way out in the sticks in the desert parts of Nicaragua who lives and struggles and reflects and prays and works with her community. These are the people in whom already the kingdom is alive. The risen life is already happening in them, the resurrection is in their flesh, in their lives'.

    These people are the kingdom, the kingdom that is within us, as well as the kingdom we have to build in society. They are the guarantee of the kingdom. They are its presence already within us. They are the cornerstone of the building of the reign of God. They're our hope, our light in the darkness. So on one hand, you know, the kingdom will never come, not in the way we would hope it would. On the other hand, it's already happening in our own lives, and both need to be kept in dynamic tension. We don't split off just into activism and we don't split off just into my own private liberation. It's both personal and political. So truly in these people, and in our own ongoing struggle for justice, we experience the light which shines in the darkness, the light which the darkness was not, is not and never will be able to overcome.

And there are moments when we taste it. There are moments when we taste and see the Lord, the love, the freedom. And there is joy. There are moments of celebration. And if we forget to celebrate the freedom that's happened in our own lives, the freedom that's happening in our communities, the freedom that is happening whenever two or three people come together and commit themselves to the struggle for justice, if we fail to celebrate, in some sense we fail to realize the presence of the reign of God already with us. Let's taste, let's rejoice, let's share the beauty of the liberation that is already happening in us, in spite of the gods of this culture, in spite of the prisons and the dungeons, whether they're in Nicaragua or whether they're in our own lives, the dungeons that have kept us enslaved for so long. Let's celebrate when we managed to find freedom.

In this process, however, I do believe that the contemplatives, the people who go out into the desert in very literal senses, those who do become stripped of all that one could hang on to, one could cling to, one could use to define oneself by, these people do have a very precious gift to offer to us in reflecting on what is happening in all of us and in our lives. Not that their life or their journey is in any sense totally unique and esoteric. It's the journey of everyone, but in the sense that their greater freedom, their greater space, their greater quiet, allows them to reflect and offer back to us insights into what it means to be free, what it means to come into this phase.

Also, it's important to look at some of our models. I mentioned people like Romero before. Some might use Harvey Milk as an example. Certainly the wonderful gay pastor who had a church for gay and lesbian people, for transgender people, for prostitutes in

Paris, and he was murdered by the religious right because of his activism in trying to have the European Court make statements about gay and lesbian freedom. People like that are our great models of what it means to go into death, and yet in some way live in the liberation and the memory and the joy of the people that they have served. So we need these people, and most of all of course Jesus, to give us a sense of hope and a sense of what the journey is about. I also want to say that some of our great models are people who've died of AIDS and people who served people who were dying with AIDS; these people have very literally walked the road of death, walked the road of absolute rejection, the stripping away of all that they are, becoming a pariah, a leper in our society; giving up so much of their lives and their hopes to serve those who are dying, entering into death with them. And for so many of these people, we have seen that there is a true life, a deeper love, a greater freedom that comes, which was unimaginable before this journey began.

In some ways it still sounds like madness, even when we talk about it. And these people too are our models, are our heroes, are our cornerstones of true liberation and true communion of love, which is not about just joyful ecstasies or personal mystical experiences—which so many people in the New Age seem to want, and I might add, some of the people in the Old Age, in Christian prayer, seem to want. This is the liberation of love. This walking through the desert and the darkness together, and finding somehow, in the beaten down-ness, in the pain, in all the shit and the struggle, there is freedom, there is love and there is joy beyond what we imagined.

So, what is happening in the life and the heart of a person who is coming into this phase beyond the desert and the darkness? What few words can we say about this? It's difficult to talk about this as a gay man to other gay men, and perhaps to lesbian women, because so little has ever been written about this, especially in relation to sexuality. I got really angry a few months back because I was going through some of my own stuff around what it means to be authentic, and to be on this journey and to be sexual. I thought, dammit, all these saints and all these mystics and all these people in every tradition have said so little about sex, and how it relates to the journey of communion, of union, of liberation. So little! So we're kind of left to work it out for ourselves. Perhaps this is the gift of our age, perhaps this is what our saints have to do. And we need saints; that's an invitation, and more than an invitation, a command! We need to become these saints who can do this work to pass it on to future generations. Because the old saints didn't do it, sorry, or if they did it, they didn't write about it. So what I'm going to say is an exploration, it's just a tentative foray into possibly how we might think about this as sexual gay and lesbian people. It's difficult also because this phase, of its nature, is inarticulable, and because of limitations of language, and because of limitations of my own experience, but somehow we have to say something.

I'd like to read a few verses from a beautiful old Quaker hymn, a beautiful thing, and I think this expresses almost as well as anything what is happening in the life of a person who has been through the desert and is coming into liberation. I'm sure you know the hymn, it's called 'How can I keep from singing?' Just listen to the words, and listen to them as gay and lesbian people who are coming to liberation.

My life flows on in endless song above Earth's lamentation.
I hear the real though far-off hymn that hails a new creation.
Through all the tumult and the strife, I hear that music ringing.
It sounds and echoes in my soul, how can I keep from singing?

What though the tempest round me roar, I hear the truth, it liveth.
What though the darkness round me close, songs in the night it giveth.
When tyrants tremble, sick with fear and hear their death knell ringing.
When friends rejoice both far and near, how can I keep from singing?

In prison cell and dungeon vile, our thoughts to them are ringing.

When friends by shame are undefiled, how can I keep from singing?
The peace of Christ makes fresh my heart, a fountain ever springing.
All things are mine since I am Christ's, how can I keep from singing?

No storm can shake my inmost calm while to that rock I'm clinging.
Since love is Lord of heaven and Earth, how can I keep from singing?

As I say, I know of nothing which expresses quite so beautifully what it means to be coming into this liberation. How can I keep from singing? It's grounded. It's honest. There is pain, tumult, strife, raw. And yet there is the freedom, there is the new creation. I hear it echoing in my soul. How can I keep from singing? In the midst of all the pain, how can I keep from singing? It's also political: tyrants who hear their death knell ringing; friends, even in dungeons, even in pain and in torture, who yet are free, who are unbound. And because of them, how can I keep from singing? It's also the tasting of that spring. Remember we spoke in the second session about the spring of living water, in sexuality and in spirituality, that as it grew deeper flowed and became one. Finally, in this phase, that spring has become a fountain welling up to eternal life within our own heart, as Christ promised it would. And we taste that water of freedom, that water of life, which is the divine life in our sexuality, in our spirituality, in our action, in our contemplation, in all that we are, and how can we keep from singing?

So, this person who's coming out of the darkness is hearing the herald, the song, the trumpet, the sound of this song of freedom in their own heart, in their own guts. But at the same time, it's like Israel coming into the land of Canaan. They won a few battles and then they lost a few battles, and then they won a few more battles and they lost a few more battles. It's not all at once. Sometimes we expect we're going to come into the promised land, and everything will be rosy and fine, and we'll be happy, happy, happy. No, it's two steps forward, one step back all the way; we make it and then we fall back a bit. We get a little bit of political clout and we lose it. We get a little bit of personal freedom and then we discover how enslaved we still are. But we're getting there little by little, poco a poco, as the Latin Americans say.

And the truest sign of this is that, where there was deep pain, the pain we talked about in the desert and the darkness, now there is a deep sense of peace. The pain of being purified of all our mess and of all the false gods gives way to a quiet sense of peace. In this peace, we are indeed touching bottom. In the midst of pain (in this phase that I'm talking about now as we're coming out of the dark, there is still pain) we begin to touch a tiny seed, a tiny core somewhere at the bottom point of who we are. We begin to discover a sense of who we are. And this is the pearl of great price. This is the treasure hidden in a field. And there is the sense that no matter what it's taken in our life to reach this point of touching this fine point of bottom, of who we are, it was worth it all, even in the midst of struggle and pain. We're touching it, we're touching it, we're sensing the truth within us. Tentative, very tentative at first.

Merton says that the true self (which is who this is) hidden in God is like a shy, wild animal that only peeps out and shows its face when everything else is quiet, at rest, and silent, and all the noise and all the gods we've served, all the attempts to be someone, have become silent. The true self like a shy wild animal begins to show its face, we begin to see it, we begin to get a sense of who we are. Merton, in talking about this true self, is very much at one with Carl Jung who said that he knew of no word or concept for the deep self that is not also a word or concept for God. And Merton says, 'I cannot hope to find myself, my true self, anywhere except in God.'

There is only one problem on which all my existence, my peace and my happiness depend. And it's not about defeating the gods of the culture. It's not about political activism, though that may be a fruit. The problem, the issue, is to discover myself in discovering God. If I find God I will find myself; if I find my true self, I will find

God. So as we let go of God, as we saw in the desert, we let go of God (we pray God to rid us of God, and to go even into a darkness beyond God), what we do find is our true self, this tiny hidden core, fragile, yet unmistakable.

It seems to me absolutely crucial, absolutely central that in this coming into my true self, obviously I absolutely have to come into my true sexuality, into the fullness of who I am as a sexual being. There can be no true self without that. And in fact, for a gay and lesbian person especially, but probably for anyone in our culture who has denied and repressed sexuality so much, coming into a full owning and living of who I am, rejoicing in who my sexual self is, is the royal road into the true self. Because it will cause us to destroy and throw away all the gods and the self-definitions that our culture throws onto us, all the stuff we have taken in and defined ourselves by, it will smash them and lead us through them if we will follow our sexual desires, our sexual needs, even our sexual fantasies; the truth of who we are as sexual beings will lead us to the truth of who we are as beings. So there's no question here of in any way sexuality being peripheral. It is at the heart of coming into who we truly are.

So slowly, tentatively, we come into this quiet silent space, still not free, still in pain, but becoming free, this tiny point, which becomes our touchstone. And gradually all of our life will be referred to this touchstone. We'll see that as we go on. It's crucial here to have discernment as we hear this, as we touch this tiny point. It's good to have help and someone to companion us in this journey. At times there is a profound joy in this. It's very quiet. It's very silent. It's a deep breathing from within. It's not yet celebration, but there's a sense of 'Oh, my God, I can breathe.' At last I know what it is to breathe, deep in who I am.

I want to read you something again from Merton. Merton's a great guide through this for modern people. I want to say by the way that I think a lot of the models and guides we've been given in this phase of communion with God, which is what this is about, the guides from the past, including the middle ages, especially the middle ages, they don't cut it anymore. Somehow they don't speak our language. Someone like Merton I think does. Merton says this, I love this quote.

> At the center of our being is a point of nothingness, which is untouched by sin and by illusion, a point of pure truth, a point or spark which belongs entirely to God, which is not at our disposal (you know, if we tried to muck it up, to mess it up, we couldn't), from which God disposes of our lives, which is inaccessible to the fantasies of our own mind, or to the brutalities of our own will. This literal point of nothingness and of utter poverty is the pure glory of God in us. It is, so to speak, God's name written in us, as our poverty, as our sonship, as our daughterhood. It is like a pure diamond, blazing with the invisible light of heaven. It is in everybody. And if we could see it, we would see these billions of points of light coming together in the face and blaze of the sun that would make all the darkness and cruelty of life vanish completely. I have no program for this seeing. It is only given. But the gate of heaven is everywhere.

This little point of nothingness, of absolute poverty, is the pure glory of God in us. How privileged, how gifted we are as gay and lesbian people: if we can go into our poverty, into our exile, into our rejection, into our nothingness, we can find this pure point of nothingness, this poverty, which is the brilliant diamond, the diamond of God's own life. I won't make a joke about it, but I can't help but reflect that our culture can bastardize even something like this, when someone like George Bush can talk about a thousand points of light: what an obscenity. This is the thousand points of light that is true light, that is truly the life of God. The Gate of Heaven is everywhere.

So, as we come into this deeper and deeper awareness of this point of life, this point of nothingness, as it comes to be who we are, what happens? I love this, I love this part. The first part is the one who is in exile comes home, in fact finds that he has been at home all along, the home within. This is a home which no one could ever give to us. The home which is us. We find we are not in exile, we belong. In Scripture it says, 'Those who are called not a people, I will call my people.' That's us. We were called no people, no one's people, the scum. And now we're called 'my people'

The exile finds home deep within, and all the tentacles that we've sent out throughout the world, searching for home, searching for something to make us feel we are worth something, searching for love, searching for belonging, all these tentacles come home. And we find we are already there. It's already in us. And this belonging is a belonging not just within me, it's a belonging to all creation. I find that I also belong, I'm also at home with every creature, with every being, no separation, no exile for anyone, for any being, absolute belonging to all creation.

And so this interdependence, this sense that I am part of this web, which is the whole of life, I have a place here, I have a right to be here, is given to me by this God who is who I am. This beauty I see all around me, and it expresses itself in solidarity with all beings. Each of these realizations within has an expression in the world outside us, which is also profoundly political. And the expression outside us is solidarity, solidarity with all beings, with every creature, with every human being. We know what the human condition is and we share that with everyone, including those who oppress us. We share it also with all beings. And we are particularly in solidarity with all those who are most oppressed, who are most told they don't belong, who are most told that they are in exile, because we know that place so well. So they especially are the ones we are in solidarity with.

Secondly, the one who was broken, the one who was fragmented, the one who was at war with himself or herself, especially the one who had been told that sexuality and spirituality had to be in absolute conflict with each other, this broken one becomes whole, this broken one becomes one, and begins to taste union and integration. Gradually all the fragmented parts of the personality start to come into unity around a single center. All the competing forces within us that wanted attention, that wanted to be served, whether it was ambition or career or so-called love, or making it in some form, being someone, getting the right wardrobe or the right goods, whatever it was that vied for our attention and our energy now comes into unity around the single center and becomes subject to the true center. This person is becoming whole. Each of those parts is welcomed and affirmed for its own goodness, its own beauty, and what it can contribute to the whole person. It's also a place of great harmony. It's a place where we have a sense of justice, especially to those parts which were most degraded, most put down within ourselves. We now welcome them back within us and accept their gifts most reverently. They are the parts to whom we give the most honor now.

And this will be expressed in the world as justice, as a concern for the good of everyone, but especially those who have been most oppressed and denied justice. Now, we will see them as deserving the greatest honor, just as those degraded parts of ourselves, usually our sexuality, deserve the greatest honor now in this unified person, this unified whole. And in this, there is a great sense of peace, a great and deep sense of peace. The person is coming home, the person is becoming themselves and they are becoming one.

There's a beautiful story in Randy's Shilts' book *And The Band Played On* where he traces the journey of one particular gay man in the Castro in San Francisco who develops AIDS. I can't remember his name, but a beautiful man who was well-loved and had a lot of friends and did a lot of active work in the community. When he first gets AIDS, he goes through this process of discovering what a beautiful spiritual teacher it can be; he's full of joy and delight in the expansion and the lessons he's learning. Then he goes through this profound experience of death and darkness, where he says, 'There is nothing beautiful about AIDS, it's ugly, it's disgusting, it's death, it's putrid, it's obscene.' The awakening, then the desert and the darkness. And finally, when he's dying, Randy Shilts is saying that people are visiting his deathbed as if it were a holy shrine. And a friend goes in and talks to him and says, 'What is this? What's going on here? All these people are coming to you as if just being with you is like somehow touching the holy.' This guy who is on his day of death, as far as I can remember, says, 'You know, I finally get it, I finally get it. I am light. And I am love. And I transform other people simply by being myself.' This is what this person is learning in this phase, to simply be himself.

Thirdly, the slave, the one who was in slavery, is becoming free. The one who was enslaved to society, to the church, to his family, to his own old sense of self, to dictate his values, his needs, his desires, his possibilities, what he could be, what he could not be, the one who relied on all these outside forces to judge him, to condemn him, to restrict him, to punish him and also to reward him, to give him carrots and make him feel better, who relied on these outside gods to define who he is, to dictate who he could love, how he could love and how he could be loved, to tell him who God is and who God wanted him to be, this person is now becoming free. And all of that is coming from his own heart. No one outside now can tell this person what it means to live, what it means to love. This is the person now who is free.

Now, this is not without dialogue. It's important there be dialogue with these outside forces as well, because there is some wisdom out there. We are not total laws unto ourselves. But the touchstone now is the free touchstone of the heart. And now the person is free to hear the call of the heart. This is the person who's coming into the phase where Augustine says, 'love and do what you will'. Now there is the deep freedom within to do that responsibly, wisely, justly, lovingly, not irresponsibly, not crazily, or madly, but as the true person, truly free.

So we need to stress that these false gods have been faced and confronted in society and in oneself. This is absolutely critical. The false gods, the internalized crap, is mainly in here. This is what really enslaves us. And so this is where the true liberation has happened, is happening. The person then is also becoming free of his addictions, of his compulsions, of his fears: becoming truly free. This is expressed in the outside world as just that: freedom. You can't pin this person down, you can't make him feel guilty. It's a beautiful thing. You can't make this person feel guilty. If there's guilt or shame, it can only come from within when the person feels they have denied the truth of who they are, which we're still capable of doing at any point, but you can't get guilt put on you from outside anymore.

It's a quiet challenge, sometimes quite a strong challenge, to people around us. Because someone who's free shakes you up, makes you face your own enslavement. And of course then in relation to the wider society, this is someone like a Romero. This is someone who cannot be cowed or beaten down, no matter what you do. There's a wonderful story, which expresses the fullness of this freedom. It comes from Tibetan Buddhism. In some attack on a monastery, way up in the mountains, some guy broke through the gate and raced up to this very old monk with a lance or a sword drawn. And the old monk simply stood there, quietly smiling. And the guy stopped in his tracks and got very aggressive and said, 'What's wrong with you old man? Don't you realize that I'm the one who could run you through without batting an eyelid? The old man said, 'And don't you realize that I'm the one who could let you run me through without batting an eyelid.' This is a person who is free of guilt and free of fear, a very dangerous person.

So, they're the three key things I think are happening here: the exile coming home and expressing that in solidarity; the fragmented one becoming whole and one and expressing that in justice; the slave becoming free and expressing that in free action in the world.

Underneath all this then is this profound journey, which is one, even though I've given it three, and I will give it yet another, context/concept. In the center of this is deep, deep surrender. And there is also pain. Because what is happening, Rumi says, is like the spokes of a wheel; the true self is down here, like the center of the spokes. This center is turning around and the spokes are severing all attachments, cutting off attachments to all the old false gods and false values that enslaved us and made us a prey for the culture around us. This is profoundly painful. This is not an easy process. At this stage, the person is still feeling the rub, is still feeling the cuts. It's not easy, because we still long for so much of what the culture gave us, including what our gay culture gives us. And most profoundly, like Jesus in the garden of Gethsemane, we don't really want to die. And yet we are dying, we know we will go through death and we feel the pain of that.

I want to say that this severing of attachments is also a severing of who we may have thought we were sexually. And so sometimes the person who may have become comfortable with one sense of being gay or lesbian finds that they need to go deeper into that, that there are issues and areas in their sexuality not yet plumbed, not yet depthed. And they have a lot to learn from people who they may have regarded as sexual outlaws, to walk in sexual ways that are frightening even for them. So this too can be a severing of the old sexual self we thought we had become comfortable with. Nothing escapes this turning around the center of the self, as the person is actually freed. But this freeing is, as I say, a painful process.

As this process goes on, there'll be times when there is great struggle and great strain and tension. And there'll be times when the person feels as if the center is not going to hold, as if one's going to lose it. Now, in the early stages of this process, occasionally one does lose the center, and then find it again, and then lose it again. But gradually, the center begins to hold. And in spite of the most painful moments of struggle and of purification, of letting go, of lostness, of confusion, of emptiness, somehow underneath it all in the silence, the center remains, it holds. And this is the most crucial stage. This is becoming an abiding reality within us. The center now is not just something that shows its face every now and then, it is becoming a continuous presence. And we can continually sink down into it and use it as our touchstone all the time. So when we start to find, however obscurely, that in the midst of our pain and confusion, there is still this point which is present (and we can access it, not always with our mind, but somehow it's there), it allows us to let go of things we would never have dreamt we would let go of, all our securities. And we know we will continue to do that. This is when the person is going deep in the spiral and coming into what can be called the unitive way, to use the old expression from Christian spirituality, coming into a subtle embryonic union with God. It's been reached.

And for those who are conversant with this terminology, I just want to say that what we've forgotten in Christian spirituality is that the unitive way is a way, it is not simply a state. One does not simply move from the dark night into the fullness of possession of God, to full union; one enters onto the road of the union of love with God, as John of the Cross calls it, it is a way. The person here now, with the subtle and abiding presence of the center, which is freeing. (I'm sorry, it's just coming up in me.) It's freeing in ways we never expected it, and in ways that people around us find bewildering. Amazing. How can you do this? How can you keep going in this way? There's no security, there's no five-year plan. You're just responding to what comes from the center. What they often forget is the pain of that, the insecurity of that, the challenge of that to keep going to this place. Because this center can still be denied, we haven't reached a point yet where the center can no longer be denied, that will come later. But at this point it can be denied. So there is a constant challenge to go down into the center and to be faithful to what it calls us to.

In this phase then, one is becoming deeply receptive. There's no sense of 'I'll get out there and I'll do it and I'll make it happen and I'll work it out.' A lot of the writers talk about the way of non-action, the way of passivity even, the way of receptivity and active passivity where the person simply remains present and, in some sense, floats on God's bosom, as another writer put it. Floating, he says, is not drifting. Floating requires a certain kind of passive activity to remain afloat. It's not just drifting like a log of wood. There is a cooperation going on here, which is very challenging, very painful. So, deeply receptive, a sense of passivity, letting go … in this phase, one realizes one wouldn't know what to do anyway, recognizing I don't know where this is supposed to go. I don't know how to make the reign of God come. And recognizing also at a deeper level, there is nothing to do, there simply is nothing to do. Now, I can't explain that; those who have experienced that in however subtle a form know what I'm saying. This does not mean we don't work for justice. We do. Or that we don't continue to walk the road. We do. And yet there is nothing to do. We can simply be. In this phase we are becoming a human being truly.

Someone said, for a lot of people in Western culture, especially the United States I think, we should talk about human doings not human beings. In this phase, the person is becoming a human being very truly. I want to say that this receptivity in some sense is physical. Anyone who's experienced any sense of contemplation knows that contemplation is gut. It's not really head or even heart, although the heart is certainly involved. It is gut. It's deeply physical. Contemplation is a physical act, not only, but it is genuinely physical, and it involves our sexual center, it involves our guts, it involves our anus, it involves all that we are down here especially and becoming deeply receptive here. Now, particularly gay men are going to hear a lot of sexual talk in what I'm saying, deeply receptive. I think this is one of the gifts of gay men in this phase, that we can be receptive. It's not as agonizingly painful as it might be for straight men. It's still painful, but perhaps we have learned something about receptivity, something which I do believe many women already know in very many ways with that often deep receptive capacity for the female; we are experiencing that too as gay men. And I sometimes think this is a physical reality, literally; through our loving in physical ways. God is opening us up and making us more receptive to the penetration of God into our bodies, into ourselves, into our deepest center, into our heart. Here one finds where one may have wished to penetrate God, now one wishes to be penetrated by God, to utterly receive God. Around this phase, there can be a sense of plateau; one has reached this point, and where the hell do I go from here, what happens next? One can only wait, wait and trust that somehow God will come into us, will respond to this deep receptivity that is also physical.

So waiting, trusting, not knowing, being free, but feeling the pain, remaining in the darkness, asking (very important) that God will come into us. And one discovers firstly that one cannot be open enough. In some sense, God has to do the opening. And now all at once the tables are turned. When we're at the moment of deepest receptivity, of deepest awareness that we can't even be open fully ourselves, yet asking God to come and be in us, at this deepest point of receptivity, of vulnerability and of knowing that we ourselves can't ever be fully open, we need God to do that for us, and of asking (it's critical that we ask for this openness and this receptivity, as well as asking that God may fill us), at this point suddenly the tables are turned. And what we discover is that the lover, the divine lover, is asking me, is asking us, is asking you to become the lover, and to enter him, to enter God, to become the lover. And God becomes the beloved, the one who opens and receives us into his body, calls on us to be the love.

I think here of a wonderful story of the monks on Mount Athos; their great desire is to become the one who is kissed by God, a beautiful image. But here, the one who desires that, finds that he or she is asked to become the one who kisses, the one who makes love to

God. And this, I think, is most beautiful. This is the heart of it all. Because at this point in the journey, the one who was unloved (think about our stories, gay and lesbian people), the one who was unloved is now loved. The one who was forbidden to love and told that his or her love was obscene, was an atrocity, was a condemnation to hell, this one is now asked for his love, is now asked for her love, is now asked to become the lover. The tenderness of the divine lover, who enters into that deepest wound. We were told our love was shit, our love was sin, and now God asks for our love, to enter into God. This is profoundly transforming. And at this moment, by the way, you may even hear it, we are having a thunderstorm around this room. So we praise God for the thunder and the lightning and the rain. This moment is profoundly transforming on all levels of the personality. I want to read you a poem which is itself a bit of a thunderstorm, a thunderstorm to our culture, to our church. It's very old and it comes from one of the greatest theologians and mystics of the Eastern churches, one of the greatest mystics in Christian history, called Simeon the New Theologian who lived around the 10th century. And I invite you to hear this with juice, with your body, not just your soul, to hear this as a gay man, to hear this as a lesbian woman, to hear this as someone who is embodied in their sexuality.

> We awaken in Christ's body as Christ awakens our bodies. And my poor hand is Christ. He enters my foot and is infinitely me. I move my hand and wonderfully my hand becomes Christ, becomes all of him. For God is indivisibly whole, seamless in Godhead. I move my foot, and at once Christ appears like a flash of lightning. Do my words seem blasphemous? Then open your heart to him and let yourself receive the one who is opening to you so deeply. For if we genuinely love him, we wake up inside Christ's body. We're all our body, all over. Every most hidden part of it is realized in joy as him, and he makes us utterly real. And everything that is hurt, everything that seemed to us dark, harsh,

shameful, maimed, ugly, irreparably damaged is in Him transformed and recognized as whole, as lovely. And radiant in His light, we awaken as the beloved, in every last part of our body.

This is what it means to kiss God, and to be kissed by God. Who is this Christ? Who is this Christ that I am asked to love, that I'm asked to enter with my own body, make love to? Is this the Royal bridegroom, as the Middle Ages would talk about him? The nuptial couch, the secrets of love? Is this the Christ of the church, is this the cosmic Christ? So who is this Christ that we are asked to love? The Christ I believe, more than believe, that we are asked to love in our time is the crucified Christ, not the cosmic Christ, the risen Christ, the royal bridegroom. We are asked to make love to the crucified Christ on the cross as he dies, to enter him in some way with our body, certainly with our heart, and make love to him, in that place of pain, of rejection, of being an outcast, being thrown away, in that place of dying, a place of anguish and abandonment. And in that place of pleasure is where we are asked to make love to Christ.

Today is the feast of St Francis of Assisi, as we are recording. I would like to show you an icon of Francis that comes from an old Spanish painting that has been reworked by a Jesuit priest in Albuquerque. It's what we see in this icon, which by the way was painted by William Hartnett Nichols, who has done a lot of work with people with AIDS. He has taken this painting by the Spanish master Miro, and he's transformed it, which is what has to happen for us in our time around loving Christ, we have to transform the old images into ones that will speak to our hearts today. Not just speak to our hearts but challenge our hearts. So what we have here is Christ crucified being embraced by Francis of Assisi. And Francis, amongst other things, is always known for his passionate love of Christ, passionate love of the humanity of Jesus. He's often called a seraphic saint because his love for Christ was like the flame of a seraph. But it was a love for the physical human Christ who walked the earth and who cared for the lepers and who was crucified. So this image that Miro gives us is very true about Francis embracing Christ. The Christ we see in this icon is a Christ covered with kaposi sarcoma, and a Christ who, above his head, has not 'Jesus of Nazareth, King of the Jews' but 'AIDS leper, drug user, homosexual', something in our day that is far more condemnatory, far more of an outcast than even those words accusing him of being the so-called King of the Jews.

I think the icon painter is saying that the lover of Christ today (and this person at this point in their journey is surely that) has to embrace the Christ who is the outcast, the reject, in physical ways, in very real ways, and make love to that person in their pain, in their suffering, in their rejection, and risk becoming one with them. Francis, when he first embraced lepers, was terrified of becoming a leper. The turning point of his life was when as a young man he first embraced the leper and risked becoming one. And here he is embracing, making love to, the leper Christ, and risking becoming one of those people, becoming the leper Christ himself. You also see in the image that Francis has wounded hands himself. So Francis shares the very wounds of Christ in his hands, in his feet and in his side. When Francis receives what is called the stigmata, the five wounds (he was the first person in history to ever experience this extraordinary phenomenon towards the end of his life), he had gone to a high mountain and prayed for two things. He prayed that he might receive, he might share in, the suffering that Christ went through on the cross. The person in this stage loves so much that he or she no longer asks to be spared suffering. They are willing to accept suffering. And I think as the love deepens to the love of Francis, they even ask to share in the suffering of Christ, which is the suffering of the world. The person now is not running away from suffering anymore. But he then also asked to experience the love that Christ had in his heart that prompted him, that urged him, that forced him to go through that suffering for the whole of the world.

And the answer was that he became himself, one flesh with the crucified Christ.

So this communion of love with the crucified Christ I absolutely believe has to have physical dimensions to it; it's the core of the most profound spiritual experience, but it also must have a physical dimension to it. This communion is a communion of love, which makes the two one flesh. This is the ancient metaphor of marriage, which is what making love to the Royal Christ used to use as its terminology, the mystical marriage. Well, making love with the crucified Christ is also marriage and it makes us one flesh with him. And this means in some way, in our own bodies, we need to share, we will share, in the suffering as well as in the love. But the love is so intense now, we accept the suffering.

But I want to say something about the nature of this communion and the nature of this metaphor of making love. This metaphor of making love has been castrated and stripped of all its sexual power. It's become some kind of refined thing that maybe some weirdo saint-type mystics do way out in monasteries and convents somewhere. The point of taking up the metaphor of marriage, of sexual love, is because it is so passionate, it's so erotic, it's so immediate in its lovemaking, so immediate in its communion, that to take away that sexual dimension strips the metaphor, the image, of its whole power. At this point in the spiritual life, while in the depths of the soul there is silence, the rest of the person needs images and metaphors to have some sense of what is happening to them. And what is happening to them is utter communion with Christ. Now take away the sexual power and the metaphor is dead. And the way I want to show that to you is this; in Holy Communion, when we take the host, the bread, which is Christ's body, into our bodies, that bread becomes physically part of who we are, part of our constitution. And through that we say that Christ has literally become who we are, and we have become who Christ is. But friends, there is a more immediate physical communion that is possible. And that physical communion is lovemaking.

I want to talk about lovemaking as a gay man because I am a gay man and that's the only place I can speak from. In the lovemaking of anal sex, the entry of one body into another, the gay man goes into the inner sanctum, into the deepest part of the person, the Holy of Holies, but passes through that place that has been most shameful, most rejected, most called obscene and dirty. And it's in that very place that the lovemaking must happen, that the pleasure and the joy and the intimacy and the communion must happen with Christ and with ourselves. And in that place, which is the place of life where nourishment is taken into our bloodstream directly, the place of death where that which is of no use to us anymore, that which has died in us that we might live, is shitted away. In that place, there are no gastric juices to break down our presence. This is being very out there. Our semen as we make love with Christ passes immediately into Christ's bloodstream. Our body juices become him, and in a sense he becomes us. The communion is that intimate, and it happens in the place of deepest shame, of deepest hiddenness and of deepest vulnerability, for Christ and for us. All that was shameful, harsh, ugly, maimed, irreparably damaged, now becomes holy, radiant and light as we awaken as the beloved in every last part of our body. If we truly love Christ, we wake up inside Christ's body. So said Simeon the New Theologian.

In this place, suffering and glory, suffering and joy, are almost one. St Therese of Lisieux who was dying of consumption at the age of 24 (with no drugs, no medication, going through the deepest painful physical agony) says, 'In some way, I can no longer suffer anymore because all suffering has become sweet to me.' St John of the Cross says, 'Suffering matters nothing to me. Glory matters nothing to me. Only love, only love, only love.' In this place, the pain and the pleasure, the joy and the suffering are almost one in the fullness of love. And so we make love to the crucified Christ as he suffers and dies, age after age after age, in person after person after person who comes into our life.

Now in this place, the person who is entering into this discovers and has discovered that he or she is empty of this love. This is the love he's called to, born for, that his whole being has been crying out for every moment of life, and in every lovemaking he's ever experienced. But he finds he does not have this kind of love. And so he has to wait, she has to wait, in silence for the love to be given to one's heart. And somehow in the waiting, what springs up is what John of the Cross calls the living flame of love. This is the very love of God, the uncreated, immediate fire of God's love, welling up in the person's heart, which will love the person into Christ, and unite the person into Christ, and burn away all the dross of self and self-seeking and ego; anything that's left will simply be consumed in this fire of love. And this is also the phase then in which this flame of love may burn through the person and send the person out into the marketplace again, to serve and to love in the broken and the crucified Christ in literally physical ways. There is this tradition in Christianity and in other religions that the one who has reached this peak of being transformed into Christ, or this depth of being transformed into Christ, is then sent back to wear out themselves in loving in literal, physical ways.

This love, this entering into the darkness of Christ's body is the deep communion of love, which is the Trinity itself. As St John in his gospel says, 'Anyone who loves me will keep my word, and my Father will love him, and we will come to him and make our home within him.' As we are united with Christ, we are united with God himself, with God herself, with the Father, Son and Spirit, we come into the very love of the Trinity itself. And this is the fullness of Christian mysticism, Christian spirituality. This communion of love is the source, the essence, the lifeblood, the destiny of all that is created, of everything that has ever existed. This is its destiny. This communion of love needs no justification, needs nothing to make it worthwhile, needs to do nothing. This communion of love is its own purpose and its own end and it exists only to generate and to draw everything and everyone into a deeper and deeper communion of love. In this communion of love, each person, Father, Son and Spirit is equal, distinct, seeing fully the one in the other, so that ultimately in love, there is only one being. And here the person who's come on this long journey, this beautiful journey of death and resurrection, of love, of life, is truly sharing in the divine nature, as we read in the letter of Peter. The person is becoming divinized. 'God became human so that humans might become God,' says St Irenaeus. And in the mass, we read, 'May we come to share in the divinity of Christ, who humbled himself to share our humanity.' This is what is happening in this person, in this gay and lesbian person who has gone the full journey. At length, even beyond this communion of the Trinity, one is drawn into the absolute silence and void of God, beyond even the Trinity. As Eckhart tells us, there is a silence and a ground of being, a wasteland and a void, even beyond the Trinity. And it's there that the soul finds its final resting place.

What is left to say? Sex in this period … who knows, honest to god, who knows? I would suggest that like prayer in this period, it's becoming our teacher, it's becoming our guide, it's becoming a way of truth, of honesty, of simple communion with other human beings, of finding our integration. It also grounds us in our humanity; our sexual urges and loving and relating help us not to spin off into some kind of ethereal, mystical trance state. It makes us physical human beings as Christ was, as Francis was, as the love is and must be. It keeps us present to ourselves and to other people. We are human beings. Sexual relating, I think, rather than becoming fireworks, not so much ecstasies, but it becomes very simple, very clear, very present, a simple and deep being with the other person in communion. And of course it has to become increasingly reverent, recognizing Christ and God in the other person and in myself. So sexual relating becomes deeply reverent and it leads increasingly to a deeper and deeper communion of love. Love comes up and opens the heart more and more in whatever sex we have in this phase. Ultimately, of course, it will all become the communion of love.

Two final points. It seems to me that if you want a theology of gay loving, a theology of gay sexuality, a theology of gay unions, whether monogamous or polygamous, we have to look to this communion of love, coming through intimacy with Christ into the communion of love, which is the Trinity. There are wonderful theologies of love for heterosexual marriages. I think here we can find a profound theology of love in gay loving, in gay relating, in gay unions. It is the communion of love. We all are co-equal, seeing the beloved in oneself and oneself in the beloved, a union of love which generates, but is fundamentally its own end, its own purpose. It doesn't exist to make children. It exists to be the communion of love and to draw all things and every person into the communion of love. This is a theology for gay sexuality, for gay loving.

So I'd like to end with a very simple, beautiful story that comes from way back in the 12th century. It's a story of St Francis and St Clare. We tend to think we know who Francis was. He was this wonderful, passionate, strong, earthy man, deeply in love with all creation, who also was profoundly sensitive and creative. So he had a great blend of the masculine and the feminine energies in him. Clare was his alter ego. She was a woman who followed Francis and lived a life of deep poverty and surrender as a nun in one of the little churches that Francis had rebuilt when he first began his ministry. Clara means light or clarity, and she certainly was that. She lived as a contemplative nun, enclosed the whole of her life, probably never traveled outside the monastery itself, living a very simple life of prayer and hiddenness. And yet Francis saw her as the best embodiment of all that he was trying to be. They saw each other as twin flames, twin loves, and were deeply in love. But Clare was also a very strong, a very clear woman who could stop armies in their tracks, as she did at one point in her life, and was called on later as an older woman for advice by Popes and emperors: a very strong woman. She also combined the masculine and the feminine energies very beautifully in herself. And the story is (it's probably just a story because we believe Clare never left her monastery), the story is that Clare, just before Francis died, went down to have a simple meal with him down in the forest, at the tiny little church in the middle of the valley below Assisi, to share a last meal with Francis before he died. They were sitting there and Francis prepared the meal on the bare earth as was his custom. Francis began to speak about the love of God, and as he spoke, his heart became inflamed and on fire and Clare's heart came on fire, and they both fell into an absolute ecstasy of silent contemplation and presence with God, a silent communion of love, a silent meal of love. And there they stayed for several hours. Meanwhile, up in Assisi on the hill, and in Spoleto the nearby town, the people looked out and they thought the whole forest was on fire. They saw flames leaping up above the church and flames above the trees, and hundreds of them dashed down the hill to put out the fire and save the forest and save this little church that they loved so much. When they got there, all they found was Francis and Clare, absolutely united, in one, in a total communion of love, perfectly at peace and yet their love lighting up the world like an immense fire of passion.

That is what we are called to be. That is the kind of love we are called to. At times it will be ecstatic and absolutely passionate. At times it will be surrendered, empty, dry and a pouring out of ourselves. But it is our core and our birthright as human beings and as gay and lesbian people, as sexual lovers. And my friends, were we to reach this phase, this communion of love, and surely we are all on the journey, then truly what cornerstones we will be to build the reign of God in the world, the reign of justice and peace for all people, for all beings. Truly in us, in our lives, the stone which the builders rejected will become the cornerstone of the kingdom of God.

Study Guide

Gradually and, at first, imperceptibly, a turning point is reached. The journey now becomes about opening ever more fully to the graced movement of the Spirit in oneself, whilst also heeding the call to build the 'reign of God', the reign of justice, peace, freedom, and love, in the world. We discover that we are called to make love to God. Thus, the one forbidden to love is now asked by God to become the lover.

The entire journey is undertaken for the building of the 'kingdom of God'—the reign of justice, peace, freedom, and love in oneself and in the world. This has both personal and political dimensions.

The 'now and not yet' of the Reign of God. The Resurrection must come alive in individuals and communities.

Coming out of the Dark. Where there was pain, now there is peace.

Touching the 'Core'. The 'Centre' must embrace our sexuality, and also the most rejected parts of ourselves.

The Exile finds Home—expressed as Solidarity; the Broken One becomes Whole—expressed as Commitment to Justice; the Slave becomes Free—expressed as personal and political Freedom.

In the mist of pain, struggle, isolation, and sometimes hostility, the deep centre within the person 'holds' and becomes a sure abiding presence that is dim and obscure, yet somehow also clear. The person becomes deeply receptive, even 'passive', and longs only to be more open to God. This has a physical dimension.

In some way a turning point is reached. The person is now asked to make love to God. Thus, the one forbidden to love is now called, invited, by God to become the Lover.

The One we are asked to make love to is the Crucified Christ.

Reclaiming the sexual and erotic power of the spiritual metaphor of 'love-making'.

Communion of Love in the place of deepest shame and rejection.

Waiting for and opening to the Living Flame of Love. 'I live now, not I but Christ lives in me!'

The Communion of Love within the Trinity. Love is its own end.

The silence in the soul. The silent ground of the Godhead.

How are sex and sexuality experienced in this phase?

Towards a theology of gay/lesbian loving: the Communion within the Trinity.

The holy meal of St Francis and St Clare.

'The stone rejected by the builders has become the cornerstone'.

Questions for discussion and reflection

1. Are there individuals or communities in which you have encountered the 'Resurrection', true spiritual maturity, the 'New Life' in Christ? Have you experienced this, even momentarily, in yourself?

2. 'The Exile finds Home. The Broken One becomes Whole. The Slave becomes Free'. Which image touches you most deeply, and why? Where are in your own growth towards 'home', 'wholeness', and 'freedom'?

3. Consider the areas of your life and your inner self that you find most 'shameful', 'ugly' and 'maimed'. What is the Word and the Will of God for you in these areas? Can you imagine, allow, embrace the idea of Divine Love waiting for you in precisely these areas within you?

4. Have you experienced the sense of being forbidden to love? Who forbade this? How deeply did you take this in? Can you believe that this is the very love that God asks of you as you mature in your life as an LGBTIQ+ Christian?

5. Consider your thoughts and feelings regarding the sexual imagery of making love to Christ. What is the deepest image for you personally of full spiritual union with God? What other physical/sexual/erotic imagery might be powerful or helpful for you?

6. If you are a lesbian woman, whether transgender or cis, how have you related to the traditional images of union with Christ? What images of Divine Love touch you most deeply? Does the image of making love with Sophia—Holy Wisdom, or with the Holy Spirit, hold any power for you?

7. 'Loving the Crucified Christ'. Where, in our societies and in our churches, do you see Love's crucified image? In what part of yourself? What might it mean for you to 'make love' to Christ in these people, these situations and these aspects of your hidden self? What feelings arise in you as you consider this invitation?

8. 'We need our mentors, guides, our LGBTIQ+ saints'. Do you agree? Do you know any? How would you recognise them? What qualities would they have? How would they differ from traditional, canonised saints?

9. What is your own deepest spiritual call as an LGBTIQ+ person of faith, as you perceive it, at this stage in your life? How are you

handling it? How do you imagine this unfolding in your life as you look ahead?

10. Why is the status quo in church and society threatened by the spiritual journeys of LGBTIQ+ people? How are we called to build the 'Reign of God'—the reign of justice, peace, freedom, and love? How are you being called here, now, today?

6

The Road from Emmaus

Welcome to our sixth and final session in this series. I'm conscious as we begin that we've been on a long and deep journey together. In our fifth session, we concluded our reflection on the paradigm of Christian spirituality and the journey from Exodus through the desert to the promised land. In this sixth session, I'd like to walk with you through a meditation on one of the great gospel stories. So, before we begin, let's just take a moment to place ourselves in the presence of the one the gospel stories speak about, the risen one, who really is in our hearts, my heart as I speak, your heart as you listen, and makes us one in this moment.

*

Lord, may your love be on our lips, in our hearts, in our minds, that we may truly hear and receive your good news. Amen.

*

So as I was saying, we've looked at the great story of Exodus, and the Passover, and the desert and the promised land as a paradigm for Christian living. But of course, always the great paradigm for Christians is the death and resurrection of Jesus. So we need to also reflect on, 'What does resurrection faith mean today'? Different communities have reflected on what the death and resurrection of Christ mean for them in their context and in their time, and we need to do the same thing. As I was saying in our first session, the treasury of the Scripture, the word of the Scripture, and also all of Christian tradition and history, is there for us to appropriate and to make our own story, to enlighten and enliven our journeys. This has not been done for us in a way that it is often done for people by the official church, because we're gay and lesbian people. And we don't have a place in this story, as we're told many, many times. So we have to do it for ourselves. We have the skill, we have the learning, we have the courage, we have the spirit with us to do that. So what I would like to do today in this session is to take up one of the best loved gospel stories, the story of the journey of two disciples on the road to Emmaus, and to meditate on that with you, as a paradigm for the life journey of a gay or lesbian Christian.

Firstly, just a couple of things about the Gospels and about the resurrection accounts. Some of our more fundamentalist friends both inside and outside the mainstream churches have spent a lot of time trying to match up the four accounts, as if they were going to get a clear blow-by-blow description of just what happened. So, particularly in relation to the Sunday of the resurrection, they try to work out what time he rose and what time the angels appeared and what time the women came, and it gets quite crazy. You start to have angels coming and going and stones rolling backwards and forwards, because the four stories don't fit. The details of the four accounts of the resurrection don't fit into a historical chronology. In fact, what we have are four self-contained accounts; they share some material, but basically they're four self-contained accounts, telling stories about the resurrection of Jesus, and putting them in the theological context of the writer of that particular gospel.

As we know, each of the writers had a particular theology, a particular way of understanding the life and death and resurrection of Christ, which he, maybe she, was trying to communicate to the people. And they shaped things and told stories in such a way as to communicate that theology. They also had particular communities that each one was writing to, and the communities were different. As we all know, we tend to shape our story to fit our audience; it's a perfectly healthy, normal human thing to do. We don't write in a vacuum. So, when we come to the resurrection accounts, we see the most crucial stories of all, stories of the risen Jesus, stories which impinge on history, but are also outside of history. And the gospel writer is trying to shape those stories with his own theology and for his audience. So we really don't need to look at each one to compare them too much, but to try to understand what the individual gospel is saying to us with that particular set of resurrection stories.

The Gospel of Luke is where we find the Road to Emmaus, and it's the only one that has this particular story. Now, in taking up the story and working with it, I'm doing what people have been doing since time immemorial, taking the Scripture and making it my own, making it our own. This is often called a hermeneutic, or a principle of interpretation. It's coming to the Scripture with a particular framework, a particular mindset, and saying, 'How can this story speak to me in my situation'? A classic one today is a feminist hermeneutic. So feminists, for example, are saying that the scriptures have been interpreted for 2000 years from a basically male and fairly patriarchal mindset. Let's come at them with a feminist approach and see what they can say to us in our situation, reading them and interpreting them and mining them as feminists. This is a very valid, appropriate and necessary thing to do. Well, in the same way, we as gay and lesbian people need to come to the Scripture and do the same thing for our community. And that's what I want to do with you today. I bring with me learning and a lot of experience in doing this, but it's something that each of us can also do for ourselves. We do need to do a little bit of study and reflection, well a lot of reflection, but the scriptures are primarily there to speak to our hearts. So we all have the right to do this, indeed the demand of the spirit to do this, to take up this book, and make it speak to our lives, allow it to speak to our lives.

So firstly, to look at the Gospel of Luke. Luke, whoever Luke actually was, was almost certainly not a Jew. He was almost certainly a Gentile, a Greek, probably traveled with Paul. And he is writing for a community that is primarily non-Jewish, for a community of Gentiles, Greeks probably (he writes in Greek), who were in that sense outside the traditions of the Israelites. So he's often at pains to explain Hebrew traditions and religious customs to the people he's writing to. He's also very sensitive to the role of women, and often sensitive to the place of outsiders, because his people as Gentiles were outside of Israel, and had been seen traditionally as not part of the club in any sense. Now they were Christians, and how did they fit in when most of the Christians were Jewish; those sorts of things are very much on his mind when he's writing.

The resurrection account that Luke gives us is only one single day; it starts on a Sunday morning, and it flows straight through into the Ascension. That's really only one day, and there's really only one story. There's a reference to the women going to the tomb, and the angels appearing and saying, 'He's not here, he's gone to Galilee', but they don't see him. The women then go back to the apostles who are gathered with 'all the others', so there are other people there in Luke's story. And the women tell the apostles and the others what they've heard and what they've seen with the angels. But Luke says, 'the other women with them also told the apostles, but this story of theirs seemed pure nonsense, and they did not believe them.' So the apostles don't believe them. Peter, however, went running to the tomb. Peter goes in and sees the cloths and is amazed at what's happened. But he also does not see Jesus. We then have the story of Emmaus, the two disciples on the road, and Jesus meets them, and we will go into what happens later. But all this happens in one day. It's really one single story.

This community that Luke was writing for, the community of Gentiles, also had a concern about the cross. One of the great issues in the early church was how to explain the crucifixion of Christ. This was seen as a great scandal, a great tragedy. This ought not have happened in a world ruled by the Romans in a world of Greeks. How could a 'god' or a 'son of god' possibly have to go through this kind of experience? This is a total catastrophe. So, a lot of the preaching in the early church, and a lot of the writing, is to try to explain that the cross was not a mistake, it was not a tragic mistake, it was not the ultimate disproving of Jesus' message but, in fact, the opposite. It was the verification, the validation of who Jesus was. This was not an easy task. The cross was a great scandal. So that's also on Luke's mind as he's writing for these people. Given all that, let's look at the actual story. I'll read it through with you, and be very conscious of all the little bits and pieces; many of us know the general outline of the story but there's a lot more in it than we often imagine. I'm reading from the Jerusalem Bible version.

> That very same day, two of them were on their way to a village called Emmaus, seven miles from Jerusalem. And they were talking together about all that had happened. Now, as they talked this over, Jesus himself came up and walked by their side, but something prevented them from recognizing him. He said to them, 'What matters are you discussing as you walk along'? They stopped short, their faces downcast. Then one of them called Cleopas answered him, 'You must be the only person staying in Jerusalem who does not know the things that have been happening these last few days.' 'What things,' Jesus asked. 'All about Jesus of Nazareth,' they answered, 'who proved he was a great prophet by the things he did and the things he said in the sight of God and of the whole people, and how our chief priests and our leaders handed him over to be sentenced to death and had him crucified. Our own hope had been that he would be the one to set Israel free. And this is not all. Two whole days have gone by since it all happened. And some women from our group have astounded us. They went to the tomb in the early morning, and

when they did not find the body, they came back to tell us they had seen a vision of angels who declared he was alive. Some of our friends went to the tomb and found everything exactly as the women have reported. But of him they saw nothing.' Then he said to them, 'You foolish men, so slow to believe the full message of the prophets. Was it not ordained that the Christ should suffer and so enter into His glory?' Then, starting with Moses, and going all through the prophets, he explained to them the passages throughout the scriptures that were about himself. When they drew near to the village to which they were going, he made as if to go on. But they pressed him to stay with them. 'It is nearly evening,' they said, 'and the day is almost over.' So he went in to stay with them. Now, while he was with them at table, he took the bread and said the blessing. Then he broke it and handed it to them. And their eyes were opened, and they recognized him. But he had vanished from their sight. Then they said to each other, 'Did not our hearts burn within us as he talked to us on the road, and explained the scriptures to us?' They set out that instant and returned to Jerusalem. There they found the eleven assembled together with their companions, who said to them, 'Yes, it is true. The Lord has risen and has appeared to Simon.' Then they told their story of what had happened on the road, and how they had recognized him at the breaking of the bread.

I've ended my reading of the story at that point because that is the point where most people end the story. In fact, I think it goes on beyond that, as I'll discuss a little later. So here is this really beautiful story about these two people walking down the road together, chatting away about what's happened, feeling sad and downcast. What does this story have to say to us? What can this mean for us as gay and lesbian Christians? How do we see ourselves in this story? Well, the first thing I'd like to suggest (might seem a little bit revolutionary) is that we can very readily imagine these two disciples as two gay men or two lesbians. Why not? Apart from anything else, we know that Luke lived in a Greek world. And in the Greek world at this time, homosexuality was very common. Even gay unions were very common as John Boswell demonstrates in his new book. This was not an unknown reality. It might not have had much favour amongst the Jews or been very well known there. But amongst the Greek community, it would have been quite common. And Luke is already speaking to people, for people, who are outside the club, which was originally a Jewish club and eventually embraced Greeks and Gentiles as well. So even from that perspective, anthropologically, there is no reason why these two people could not be gay or lesbian. So let's just say that they are; in a sense, they are us and they are taking this journey. So they go along the road, and what happens?

Already they're in a reflective mode. Already they're discussing what has happened in their lives and to their hopes. So already there's a certain kind of openness. Jesus, unrecognized, comes and walks along with them. So he's a stranger who comes and walks with them and they allow him to do that. They welcome him. And he asks them what they're talking about. And in this we see it's already God's initiative, Christ's initiative, coming to our road to walk with us and ask us, What's on your mind? What's on your heart? What's happening here? Why are you looking downcast? Why are you sad? Why are you walking this road? So it's always the initiative of Christ that comes into us, even in our attempts to take this up and use this story; it is the Holy Spirit already coming to us.

They stop short. They stop. They're prepared to wait and pause and answer the stranger's question. And I think this is beautiful. They are open to the stranger. They're sad, they're downcast, they're dispirited, they're depressed. And amazingly, they tell him, they tell a stranger what the problem is. They tell their story. They talk about Jesus of Nazareth and what had happened to him. For me, this is a sense of emotional openness, a willingness to let others know what is on your mind, what is on your heart, to talk about the pain, the struggle, the disappointment. And I think you see that in us as gay and lesbian people at our best that we can welcome the stranger and be open to hear their questions, and share something of our hearts with them, especially if we feel they are genuinely interested in us. So what do they say? They talk about Jesus, and they say that he proved he was a great prophet by the things that he said and did. And that their own hope had been what? That he would be the one to set Israel free. Isn't that our hope in relation to Jesus? Hasn't that been our hope all along, that he would be the one to set us free? That in coming into communion with him, in reading the scriptures, in being part of his community, his people, he would set us free. This had been our hope. But what has happened? In this story, they say that the chief priests and their leaders took him and had him crucified. They handed him over to be sentenced to death. And there is this deep sense of betrayal that the very people who they had relied on to lead their community had been the ones who betrayed Jesus, who they had hoped would be the one to set them free. Sounding familiar?

I think this is a crucial part of what we experience as gay and lesbian people, that our leaders are the ones who betray us and betray Jesus. In a sense, they are the ones who have taken him away from us and us from him, and forbidden his freedom to reach into our lives and into our hearts, told us we have no place in it. Or if we do, it's a tiny little box called 'it's okay to be gay or lesbian, just don't love, just don't relate, just don't worship God with your bodies.' What a farce. What a betrayal. What a counterfeit of what it means to be a human being. And this is in the name of Christ. This is the great betrayal.

So, we can immediately identify with these two people, we know what that feels like, freedom has been denied us. Our hopes are dashed and we go away sad. They go away on this journey, and this journey away from the community, away from Jerusalem, that appears to them like the end of their hopes, will in fact turn out to be the true journey, the true journey in which they will encounter the risen

Christ, not in the terms of the community back in Jerusalem, but in their own lives, in their own experience. They don't know this at this stage. But something of integrity and truth has made them name the betrayal, name the unfreedom, and go out from the community on this journey, not knowing what it will lead to.

I also want to note something that I think is often missed. They say to Jesus that some of their friends had gone to the tomb and found everything exactly as the women had reported. Now we read a little earlier that when the women came back from the tomb, the apostles did not believe them. This story of theirs seemed pure nonsense. Peter went and checked it out but the apostles as a group did not. Now we discover that some of the friends of these two disciples did go and check it out. In other words, some of their friends, not the apostles, thought the women's story might be credible. Now this, I think, is very touching. These women come back with this amazing story and these men, who are the leaders of the community, the ones chosen by Jesus, don't find this story worth even getting up and leaving their Sunday breakfast for, not worth going to check out. It's just nonsense. As if, how could their story be worth anything? They just don't believe them. But this other group, some of their friends do. This also makes me suspect they're gay and lesbian people because so often there's a much, much greater sensitivity to the story that others give, and especially those who are on the outer. If it's spoken from the heart, they're much more inclined to listen to it and say, let's go and check this out. Even though it seems crazy, we'll go and see it, we'll go check it out.

And of course, they find the tomb. Everything was exactly as they had reported, the women were telling the truth, but of him they saw nothing. It's interesting that Luke mentions Peter; Peter will come up again later because, of course, we know that Peter and Paul in the early church had some discussions and arguments. In some ways, Peter represented, as he still does, the rock, the mainstream, and Paul was trying to bring in the Gentiles, the outsiders, the Greeks. Luke is doing this beautiful balancing act of telling the story of these people who went away from the community, but letting Peter emerge as in some way faithful or looking reasonably good. So Peter had gone to check it out too. The other apostles hadn't bothered.

Okay, so let's just take a look for a moment at this community that they've left and why they may have left. This community is a community where the central proclamation of the Christian faith is not received. The women come back (maybe it's because they're women, maybe it's because of what the news is that they have to tell), and it is not received, it's treated as nonsense. This is not a community that is profoundly open to the possibilities of what God can do in our lives and in history. It is not a community that welcomes the stories told by people like women. It's not a community, in other words, where the power of the resurrection can really come alive, because these people are not open even to the possibility of it. It's a community where somehow these two disciples have sensed that the risen life is not here. The freedom is not here. The proclamation of the resurrection, even though it's already been made, is not credible. It's not a community that is alive with resurrection faith. And so they leave, they walk away, not knowing where they're going or where it will lead them.

Now, folks, isn't this our story? We have been in this community, many of us for decades, many of us have become professional ministers in this community. Many of us have given our lives and our energy and our hearts to this community. Worked our guts out for this community. But somehow, at some level, we've recognized that the resurrection power is not alive. It's not working. It's not free. It's not joyous. It's not the life beyond death that we had been promised. Where is the risen Jesus? Where is the good news? And most especially, where is the good news for me as a gay man, or as a lesbian? Where is the risen life for me? In this community it's not credible. There's no juice, there's no fire. It's all conformity, regulations, rules and fitting in. And we're not welcome because we don't fit in, as these women were not welcome because they did not fit into the apostles' club. And we go away sad, downcast, betrayed, disappointed. How many times have we gone away? How many times?

Some of us go away in a very literal sense, we literally leave the church. But how many of us, even if we don't leave the church, or if it takes years to leave the church, how many times have we gone away sad, saying we had hoped, we had hoped that we would find here the risen Jesus to set us free? So, like the disciples on the road to Emmaus, we go away sad, but as we make our journey away from the community, in whatever way that happens, somehow there is someone else, other people, other journeyers, who we don't recognize as Jesus at all, at first. Often they're quite crazy people, and maybe other gay and lesbian people who are even further out there than we are and who we think are basically kind of crazy. And they come and walk by our side. There may be other Christians who have gone through this journey before us and they come and walk by our side.

So Jesus comes and walks by their side, and they welcome him, and we welcome these people into our lives. He says, 'What's the problem? What are you sad about? What are you downcast about?' And we tell our story, we pour out our hearts and we say what has happened to us, our hopes, our betrayal, our leaving of the community in sadness. And then what happens? Jesus talks to them. And the first thing I want to say here is, note their openness to hearing; their hearts are open. Who is this guy? They don't know who he is. He just comes and walks by their side and starts chatting to them. And not only do they open their story to him, but they are open to hear what he has to say to them, even though he's a stranger, he's not a priest, a Rabbi, a minister, a theologian, a chief priest, he's just this guy walking along the road. But when he starts to talk, their hearts are open to hear. And the only thing that counts for them in that moment is the truth of what he's saying and the integrity with which he says it. His authority or his status is not relevant. They are open to hear the truth in him as a human being. And if the integrity is there, and the truth is there in what he says, they receive it. And this is part of our call, and our gift as gay and lesbian people, to be able to name bullshit when it's bullshit, to be able to name truth and honesty and integrity and the true story when it's told, no matter who the speaker is, no matter what status they hold or don't hold, no matter whether they're inside the community or outside the community, no matter whether they are the chief priest or a bum we meet along the roadside. To be able to hear the truth and let that person teach us and open our hearts.

As I've been doing this meditation, I am so impressed by these two disciples. After all this time with Jesus and with all these apostles, the person they really are open to hear from is this stranger they meet along the road. These people are very, very cool. They are very, very open to hear the truth. And that's our invitation, to hear the truth as it's spoken to us. So it's not a matter of external authority. It's not a matter of learning or status. It's a matter of the integrity of the heart.

And what does he say? What he says is, 'You foolish people.' And I think there's a gentleness in that, not a condemnation. So slow to get it, you still haven't got it have you? Wasn't it ordained? Wasn't it meant to be? Wasn't it the way things have to be in life that the Christ should suffer, and through the suffering enter into his glory? That's the message. Didn't you get that yet? Hadn't you picked that up yet?' He says it to these people who have been reading the scriptures and the prophets and Moses all of their lives. And they still haven't got it. They've been listening to Jesus who talked about what may happen to him, and they still didn't get it; they who'd seen him die and heard the women tell the story of his resurrection still hadn't got it. You know, we haven't got it lots of times either. It's through suffering, it's through exile, it's through becoming an outcast and going through that, losing all the status and all the securities that we come to life, and we still don't get it, we still don't get it. And that's what he's saying to these folks. And so he goes through the Scriptures patiently, through Moses and all the prophets, explains to them all the passages throughout Scripture about himself. And he says things like, 'what about the part where they say, without beauty without majesty, you saw him, we saw him, a thing despised and rejected by all, a person of sorrows and familiar with suffering. He was despised, and we took no account of him'. He says things like that. Things like, 'I am a worm and no man; my God, my God, why have you forsaken me?' He tells them all these familiar passages and says 'this is the way it is. And if you want to follow the road into life, you have to be prepared to accept some of this stuff. To die, deeply die to yourself and to all you thought made you a person, to find who you truly are'. And this was the only way that even the Christ could come to who he truly is, the risen Lord, by going through death, through suffering, through the total surrender of self in pain and in being an outcast. It's the only way through into life.

So, this is what he's telling them, this is the message we don't want to hear. We've been looking at this right throughout our five other sessions, that the Christian call unapologetically is a call that leads us to and through the cross. And that as gay and lesbian people, in our exile, in our poverty, in our littleness, in our rejection, we are the blessed poor who are invited very immediately to go through that narrow passageway of death into true life. It's the only way you can. So you want true life? If you do, being poor in that sense, poor in the eyes of the world, is a gift. Blessed are the poor, blessed are we if we can accept our poverty. So, he tells them all this stuff. Now something happens ... this is really wild. Later, they will say, didn't our hearts burn when he started to talk like this? My heart was just on fire. How was your heart? Well my heart was on fire too, it was incredible! This does it. The stuff that happened back in the community didn't do it. And here's all the apostles, you know, the leaders of the church, the foundation stones, Peter, all the guys, here's even the first message of the resurrection coming from the angels and the women at the tomb. But it didn't do it. It didn't do it. They went away sad because it wasn't alive there. But here, from this stranger, this bum they met along the road, he talks and they burn. Why do they burn? Why do their hearts burn when he talks about the story of exile and rejection and poverty and death? Because they know that place. Because he's speaking to their experience. They know what it's like to go through that. And the message that he gives, he takes them into that place in themselves.

The same thing is happening, I hope, on this tape. You know when someone talks about something that is their story and it really touches your story, your heart kind of comes alive and you say, 'Yeah, I know that, ah God, I really know what you mean, because I've been there.' It's like that, it's that kind of connection. They know what he says because they have experienced it in their guts, as we have, as gay and lesbian people, in our guts, what it means to be without beauty, without majesty, a person despised and rejected by all, someone to make people cover their faces. We know what that's like. Today in 1994, we know what that's like. So it speaks to our spirits.

Now, the second reason why their hearts burn is because he shows them that this was the way the Christ had to enter into his glory, that this is the only way into the risen life. And suddenly that which has seemed the road to death and pain and rejection becomes the gateway to life, if we accept it and go through it with Christ. This is the pathway of the Messiah himself and we're invited to go on it with him; and their hearts come alive. So, they draw near to the village to which they were going, and he makes as if to go on. And they press him to stay with them. We have to now invite him into our lives at the deepest level. Christ, God, is never going to force himself, herself onto us. He's with us. He opens our hearts. But we also have to invite him in. We have to recognize what's happening and invite this person in. At this stage, they don't know this is Christ, all they know is that this person is telling the truth. This person is right on, he's *on* in a way that the community back in Jerusalem was not, even though at this stage, he's not Christ, he's not church, he's not priest, he's not anything, he's just this guy. But he's telling the truth. Can we do this? Can we listen for the voices around us that are telling us the truth and not bother about what status they have? If it's a priest, fine, but if it's someone you meet panhandling, or an IV drug user who's telling you the truth, that's Christ, that's the voice, that's the one we need to invite into our lives and forget these others, because this is where we're gonna find the oil, the good juice, the flame, here. So it's really letting go of all that other structural stuff, and finding what really is authentic here.

Now I love this … they ask him in, they ask him to come and eat with them. In Mediterranean societies, even still, you don't invite someone in to eat with you unless you want to be very intimate with them, it's a very intimate thing to do. You really are sharing life with that person. So to invite this street person in, which is sort of what he was, into their lives, into their home presumably, to share their meal is an act of great courage and daring. But the truth he's spoken is so real that they will do that. They invite him right into the heart of their lives. And that's our invitation, to invite this Christ, however he appears to us, right into the heart of our lives where we really live. Our true homes, the truth about who we are, what we desire, what we do and don't do; there are no double lives here. This is who we really are, no pretense that we don't like this, hate that, want this, don't want that, that we're better than we are or worse than we are, that we don't have this or that fantasy, or that we haven't done this or that in our sexual experience, that we haven't hurt this person or that person, that we haven't been greedy; there's no pretense. They invite him into their lives.

And he goes. Before that, they say it's nearly evening. Their line of convincing him to stay with them is, 'it's nearly evening and the day is almost over'. In other words, it is getting to be night. Think of what we've talked about around darkness and night in this series. It's getting to be night, and they've reached the furthest point away from the community, away from the old life they knew, away from the community that could not speak with power of the resurrection. They're at the furthest point away, and it's becoming night, the dark is coming down. And they say 'come and stay with us. It's nighttime'. They're a little fearful of going into the night without this word of truth. This person who can speak the word of truth, being with them. And in our nights, in our darknesses, in our furthest point away from the community, away from that safety we thought we knew, where we didn't find life … it's a lonely journey, a fearful journey often. At that furthest point as the night comes down, we invite him in to share our lives. We say 'come and share our table, be with us in our experience'. And he does. He does come into our table. What does he do when he comes in? The passage says he went in to stay with them. As you're probably realizing now, not too much in the gospels is in there by chance. He went in to stay with them, to abide with them, to be with them. And this is not a fragmentary, momentary thing. This is a permanent thing. He goes in to stay with them. At this furthest point away, when the darkness is coming down, and their hearts are open, he comes in to stay with us.

While they were at table (they have had their meal) he takes the bread, which was their bread, their bread. He says the blessing, breaks it and hands it to them. The bread, the bread is their lives. The bread is their experience. The bread is their love, their yearnings, their pains, their joys, their life, their table, their bread. And he takes that up into his hands the same way he took it up the night of the Last Supper. This is a direct parallel, of course, to the Last Supper. And Luke's very clear that this is what it's about. He takes up this bread of their experience, he holds it in his hands and he gives thanks for it. Now the passage says he says the blessing. The Hebrew blessing for bread does not bless the bread, it gives thanks to God, the God of the universe, for this bread. And this is what he does. He takes up our experiences as gay and lesbian people, so broken, so condemned, so rejected, so degraded and abused, and he takes up this experience which is our bread, he holds it in his hands and he gives thanks to

God for our lives, for our love, for our struggle, for our pain, for our exile, for our courage in walking the journey, and trying to keep our hearts open. He takes this bread and gives thanks to God for this bread. And in that thanks, he transforms our lives into himself. This is Eucharist here. He transforms our bread into himself. And in truth, there is no transformation because all bread is Christ, all life is Christ; it's a matter of recognizing it. He then breaks open our experience, breaks open the shell of our lives, the shell of our experiences and our lives and pains. And we see it when it's broken open for us, and that breaking open is often a very painful experience. We see what was there all along. This is the very life and love of God, that is our lives, that is our loves and our struggles and our pains and our rejection, and our craziness, and our joy, and our celebration, and our intimacy with one another. This is what was there all along, the pure love of God. And all that had to happen was this stranger had to take it up, honor it, honor it, honor it as what it is, which is life, which is love, which is truth, and then break it open. And we could see what was really there, which was and is Christ. Because when he breaks it, he hands it to them. This is not something he holds here, he breaks it open and he hands it back to them, to nourish them, to sustain them, to be bread for the journey. But this bread now is also him, Christ himself, alive and risen in them in this bread. And the word is to eat it, to take it in and let it nourish us for the journey.

And at that moment, their eyes are opened and they recognize him. And this is the moment for us. Our eyes can be opened if we are prepared to let him take it up, to take the truth of who we are, in every level of our being, let him take it up and give thanks for it and honor it and break it open. Often we're the ones who are too caught in guilt and shame and negativity and self-hatred to allow Christ to take up the bread. And then to honor it. And then to transform it and break it open as himself. Often the problem is in our self-hatred, that we won't let him do it.

So, they see him and they recognize him but immediately he's gone. He's vanished from their sight. I think that happens for two reasons. One is because he's in our lives now, we don't need the physical Jesus to sit there anymore. It's us. It's you and me, who are sitting there at this table who've taken this journey together. It's the bums we met along the road. It's even the community back in Jerusalem maybe; it's us. And we need to see the risen Christ in each other. It's also because these two people have another part of the journey to make. This is really crucial. And this, my friends is often missed, both in this story and in gay and lesbian experience. First they reflect; they stop and they reflect on what has happened, absolutely crucial. Going into an experience, experiencing it fully and then reflecting on it with open hearts as gay and lesbian Christians, not just as gay and lesbian people. And in that reflection, that's when they say, 'Didn't our hearts burn? This was real. What he said was the truth. This is wild. When he talked to us on the road and explained the scriptures to us, explained how you have to go through the death and the exile to come into life, didn't that turn us on, didn't that set our hearts on fire?' What happens next? They set out that instant and return to Jerusalem. That moment. Once they've seen this, the mandate, the urge of the Holy Spirit is irresistible. They must move, they must go on another journey. And this journey is a journey back, it's a journey back to the community in Jerusalem. What for?

When they get there, they find the eleven assembled with all their companions. And the eleven say, 'yes, it's true. The Lord has risen and appeared to Simon, to Peter'. And here again, we get this beautiful thing in Luke, that meanwhile, the Lord has appeared to Peter, but only to Peter. And there's no story about that. It's just a simple statement. He doesn't get any of the airplay that these two people who had to go away got; you can see where Luke's sympathies really are. It's with these people who had to journey away and find Christ in their own experience. But he does say Peter, who is the rock, who is in a sense the church, has seen Christ. And by the way, the verb that he uses in Greek is the one that's used most through the resurrection stories. And it's that Jesus showed himself; the power is with Jesus, he does the showing. In the story of these disciples at Emmaus, we notice their eyes were opened and they recognized him. They are empowered. This is one of the rare times in the scriptures that it doesn't say Jesus did the showing; they recognized him. In this experience, the power is handed over to them, these outsiders, to recognize him. I think we have a special gift because of our outsiderness in recognizing Christ when he's really there, in a way that people inside the safe confines of the institution don't have, because we've had to look for him outside where he, in some ways, more often is, than in the structures.

So the power has come into them. This power is with them when they go back to Jerusalem. After hearing that proclamation of the resurrection to Peter, then they told their story of what happened on the road and how they had recognized him at the breaking of the bread. A couple of points here. Firstly, those words 'at the breaking of the bread', coupled with Luke's description of the meal at Emmaus, there is no doubt that this is the Eucharist of Christ. This is the full Eucharist. As far as I'm aware, it's the only time in any resurrection story that Jesus very clearly is depicted celebrating the Eucharist. At other times he eats. But this is Eucharistic language, the breaking of the bread. He might as well have said 'the Eucharist' because that's the term that they used to use, the breaking of the bread. The Eucharist is the church. It's the community of Jesus. The classic line in early Christian theology is: the church makes the Eucharist, the Eucharist makes the church. So when Jesus met with those two disciples and shared their bread and their lives and blessed it and broke it, he made their lives Eucharist, he made them church, he made them the community of the people of God in that place, quite apart from whatever they may have been doing back in Jerusalem. They could have been having Eucharists back there. But way out here at the furthest point away, they have their own Eucharist. And it's the only time in the scripture where we see the risen Jesus celebrating the Eucharist with his people. And it's with these two outsiders.

And so they come back and they tell their story. And, folks, this is crucial. This is a hard word for a lot of us. The absolute mandate, I believe, is to go back and tell our story. First we have to walk our journey, we have to go away in whatever form that incarnates in our lives as Christians, and that can take a myriad different forms. But there was a real going away and naming of the truth in the institution, and a going away sad of heart. The welcoming on the road, the learning, the openness, the invitation, the sharing, the taking of the bread, the honoring, the breaking, the reflecting (didn't our hearts burn), and then the journey back to tell our story. Whether this story was welcomed or not, we don't know. There's no account of how they were received back by the eleven. But they had to go back and tell the story. And I believe we have to go back and tell the story to the church; the story of how we have seen him in our experience in our lives and our loves, how we have experienced him on our road of exile, and how he has shown us that that is the way to life because the institution doesn't want to hear that either. Institutions never want to hear that the way to life is through death and resurrection. Institutions want to perpetuate themselves forever and never die. That's why they set themselves up to have self-replicating bureaucracies, to make sure that they never die. This is not a message they want to hear. It is a message we have to give back to the institution. And also then, of course, the message that he is in our lives outside the community. And in how many other people's lives outside the community is he also present?

So why is it so important that we go back, that they go back, and that we go back and tell our story? The story usually ends there, as I was saying a little earlier, but that's not where Luke ends the story. Luke does not end the story at that spot; even though the Jerusalem Bible has a nice break and another little heading, Luke went right on in. You've got the eleven and you've got Peter (who the Lord has appeared to, only Peter, who is the rock of the institution of the church), and you have these two people, these two, I would say, gay or lesbian Christians who have come back after having their experience outside the community, their Eucharist. And when they tell their story (they say yes he's appeared to Simon, they say well yes, he's appeared to us too), then for the first time, and the only time in the Gospel of Luke, they were still talking about all this when Jesus himself stood among them. And he said to them, 'Peace be with you.' And it's only when these two sides come together, Peter, the rock, orthodoxy, mainstream institution, and the ones who've gone away sad and found him in their exile, when they come back and tell their story, then and only then can the risen Jesus appear in the community. Only when the two are united, both stories, whether they want to hear each other's stories or not, only when they come together and tell the stories can the risen Jesus appear, can he be truly present to the whole community. Only in that moment can he then send them out with the Holy Spirit, to proclaim the good news to the world. That cannot happen, it doesn't happen in Luke's account (which then goes on into the Acts of the Apostles) until these two are together. That's the crucial point. And I think it's clear in the text. They told their story of what had happened on the road, how they recognized him in the breaking of bread, and they're still talking about this when Jesus appears amongst them. It's quite clear, this is the turning point when the two sides are together again.

So I really believe we have to be big enough, courageous enough, free enough, loving enough, compassionate and forgiving enough, and humble enough to come back in some form and tell our story to the church, whether it wants to hear us or not. Because we want the risen Christ to appear and bring the power of the resurrection, the kingdom of God, the reign of justice, peace and freedom to all the world, in and through this community that we call church, which has hurt us so much. But it is our community, it is our people, and we want Jesus to appear; he can't appear unless we come back and tell our story.

Interestingly enough, and this is really my concluding comment about this because I think we've really reached the juice of this wonderful story. Even then, a number of the disciples don't believe it's Jesus and they think they're seeing a ghost. Now I'm tempted as a gay man to say isn't that typical, they couldn't believe he had a body. You know, 2000 years later, they still can't believe he had a body. This is still the sticking point, risen or unrisen, they still don't want to deal with the body of Christ. And I don't just mean the mystical body of Christ. I mean the physical flesh and blood, gutsy, juicy, smelly, sweaty, male sexual body of Christ. The incarnation is still the great scandal and the risen body of Jesus is the greatest scandal of all. The church still thinks it's seeing a ghost, and part, I believe, of our message to the institution is that we met this guy on the road and he was damn physical as far as we could tell. I mean he was just a guy and he wanted to come in and share our meal. We invited him in and there was no question that he had a body, that he was embodied, and a full person. So this too is part of our gift as we discover the risen Christ embodied in us, that we can bring that gift back to the very disembodied church, the very disembodied body of Christ, and say, 'Come on, let's get physical here, let's honor and reverence and celebrate the body of Christ'.

Interestingly enough, in the story of Luke, Jesus then goes on to do with the whole community what he had already done with the two disciples on the road to Emmaus. We don't know what he said to Peter, it's not mentioned, but we do know that he told the disciples on the road to Emmaus about Moses and the prophets and how you had to go through exile, death, rejection into resurrection. And now he does exactly the same thing for the whole community. In other words, the two outsiders got it first, they were the ones to get the message first. They've already heard this and received it. And now Jesus has to do it to the whole community. That's what I'm saying. I think that if we can come back and tell our story, it can be a way in which Jesus can tell the story to the whole community, and maybe they might start to get it two thousand years later: and maybe not, but we have to try.

So then in the story, they wait and later receive the Holy Spirit. It's interesting that one of the last things the risen Christ says to the whole community, after he's spoken about Moses and the prophets, saying how the Christ had to suffer and so enter into his glory, he says, You are witnesses to this. You are witnesses to this. And that's why you have to go out and tell this to the world. And I believe that that is especially said to us. We who have been in a sense forced out of the community, or have left the community, in whatever way that's happened, sad, dispirited, having named the absence of the freeing power of the risen Christ, walked our journeys, learned from whoever walks with us along the road, learned what exile means, learned what trust and openness and vulnerability mean, learned what resurrection means, invited Christ into the depths of our actual truthful experience, telling the truth, and seeing Christ honor and transform, bless and break open that experience. We who have then gone back to the community to tell our stories, we most of all who know what it means to be rejected and in exile and know what it means to come to life in that place, and find freedom in that place and find life and find God in that place, that we most of all are witnesses to this truth, this unwelcome truth, for all people in all times: the only way to true fullness of life is through surrender, and through death to self, the fundamental truth of all spiritual traditions. We are witnesses to this in our lives and in our bodies. And that is our call.

So, we really have come a long way in our journey together, and I want to conclude this meditation on the Road to Emmaus, the Road *from* Emmaus, as I like to call this. This is our book, this is our tradition, we are here. Let's take up the texts. Let's take up the traditions. Let's learn from our saints and our wise ones. Let's also learn from the bums we meet along the road in our journey as gay and lesbian people. And they're not all bums, some of them are wise and wonderful people, even though the church might think they're bums. Let's learn from them too. But let's go on our journey. Let's walk, let's move, confident that Christ truly is with us. Our journey away is only a journey to find the risen Christ more deeply in our own lives and loves and bodies, and to come back and be witnesses to that profound truth. This is the blessing. This is the call. This is the gift of the Holy Spirit in us. Let's hear it and live it. Amen.

So, I want to finish with something that's very famous from St Paul's letter to the Romans. And if you do what I've done with Emmaus with the letter to the Romans, this kind of exegetical meditation as we'd call it ... Paul's done this long rambling thing through Romans, and he gets to the end of chapter eight. And it's like he's tried to cover all his bases, and it's like, 'I may have forgotten something, so what am I going to say to conclude?' I feel a bit the same way. I've tried to cover all my bases, but what have I forgotten? So what Paul says is this: 'For I'm certain of this, neither death nor life, no angel, no prince, nothing that exists, nothing still to come, not any power or height, or depth, nor any created thing can ever come between us and the love of God made visible, made tangible, made bodily in Christ Jesus our Lord.' And I want to say, coming to the end of all that I've said, 'For I'm certain of this. All of death, all of life, every angel, every prince, everything that exists, everything still to come, every height, every depth, every created thing unites us and transforms us into the love of God made visible, made bodily, made sexual, made human, in the love of Jesus our Lord. Amen. Amen. Come Lord Jesus.

Study Guide

We are called to go forward on our journey with trust, honesty and openness, even when it seems to take us along unknown roads. We do not walk alone. As we enter deeply and vulnerably into the truth of our lives and our loving, and open to the presence of Christ within and among us, we discover a new fire and a new call. The Holy Spirit impels us to return, in some way, to the faith communities we have walked away from in despair, and to tell our story of how we have recognised Christ in our lives and our loves, in the journey away from the community, in the deep truth of our experience. Only then can the Risen Christ become fully alive and present in the whole community.

The importance of the Gospels in coming to understand Christian life for gay and lesbian Christians. The need for sound study and learning as well as reflective reading and creative interpretation.

Introducing the Gospel of Luke, and the community he wrote for.

A gay and lesbian 'hermeneutic'—or 'principle of interpretation'. We can, and we must, reclaim these scriptures for our time and our communities, and for our personal journey of faith.

'The Road to/from Emmaus' is very much our story. Imagine the two disciples as two gay men or two lesbian women, or two people who are transgender (see A note on language):

- The importance of honest and supportive companionship
- Being reflective, open to God's initiative, open to the stranger
- The journey away from the community, as a group where the resurrection has been proclaimed but not truly received
- Honesty in leaving, walking our own roads openly, vulnerably sharing our stories with one another, owning our sadness, grief, and deep spiritual disappointment

- And yet, remaining open to surprise as we walk
- Open to women, strangers, those whose witness is said to count for nothing
- Ready to speak and listen to the truth, regardless of status or structures or our own expectations
- Suffering and rejection as the road to Risen Life—the cross is the only way. Our hearts burn: we know this place. We know the lessons of the rejected ones. We hear the truth of our experience named.

Such is the potency of this encounter that we invite the 'stranger' in to share our table, our lives, our actual experience. It is our bread, our real lives and our loves that the stranger takes up, blesses and breaks open. In this, our eyes are opened and we see the One who has been with us on the difficult road we have been walking. Here, the Risen One is sharing Eucharist with his people.

In response, first, we reflect together and acknowledge our shared experience and shared revelation.

Together, we know the almost irresistible call to return and proclaim what we have experienced, especially to our still fearful and confused and grieving community. The hardships of the road and the dark of night do not deter us, such is the 'fire' within our hearts that this encounter and revelation have kindled.

We return and tell our story—of the road, of the stranger who accompanied us, and of the revelation/recognition we shared. How will we be received?

In Luke's account: 'The Lord has risen and has appeared to Peter'. They then tell their story. Thus the witness of Peter, the 'rock' of the church, and of these two 'outsiders' come together. Jesus has not yet appeared to the whole community.

Jesus appears to the whole community, breathes peace upon them. Jesus opens the minds and hearts of the whole community as he had already done for the two disciples in their journey away from the community.

He commissions the community—but tells them to 'wait in the city'—timing is important; empowerment is important.

This is how it is with us. We are called, in different ways, to 'return' and tell our story of our encounters with the Risen One—on the road, and in our own most intimate moments at 'table' with those we love.

Only when the witness of the 'outsiders' and 'Peter' come together in our time can the Christian community truly be filled with the power and joy of the Risen Christ. Our witness is essential, no matter how we may or may not be received.

We can only share our stories if we have responded to the call to walk on our own journeys, even when these seem to take us away from the official church community.

We need to walk in company, supporting and reflecting with one another. The need for genuine communities of faith for LGBTIQ+ people.

Questions for discussion and reflection

1. How and when have you 'gone away sad' from your church community? In what ways were your 'hopes dashed'? Are there different levels and various ways in which people 'go away'—perhaps even while still seeming to remain within the community? Are we called by God to 'leave'? How have you personally experienced this? How have you responded, over time?

2. How and when has the church led you deeper into the 'Risen Life' of Christ? How and when has the church failed you in this?

3. Do you really believe that the 'Cross', the road of suffering and death to self, is the only true way to life? Do you truly believe that the 'poor' are 'blessed'? How have you experienced this in your own life? Where are you still resisting this teaching?

4. Have you ever sensed the presence of God, or Christ, accompanying you on your journey, especially as an LGBTIQ+ person? Have there been 'strangers' who have walked alongside you, and who have been 'Christ' for you?

5. When have you experienced true Eucharist—the Holy Meal of Life and Love, not just 'mass'—as an LGBTIQ+ person? What was it about these moments that made them truly eucharistic for you? Have there been moments when you suddenly realised that Christ was truly present for you, especially in situations and experiences where you thought you had lost sight of God's love? How did this change you?

6. Are there areas in your life which you are holding back from Christ, not truly inviting him in to share your 'table' as it really is? Why are you keeping these areas from Christ's love? How might you grow beyond this resistance and gradually become fully open to Divine Love?

7. How do you feel about the call to 'return' and 'tell our Story'? Does the church want to hear us, to hear you? How can we live and 'tell our Story' creatively and not just in words? How can we work towards a greater dialogue within the church, not just for us but for all whose journeys, lives and stories have been marginalised, silenced or excluded by religious authorities and 'mainstream' Christians?

8. In the Emmaus Story there are two disciples, waking together. Have you had such a companion (or companions) on your path? How

important is it to walk these roads in company with supportive companions?

9. How do you feel about reflecting on Scripture in the way it is done in this lecture? Have you studied and worked with the Scriptures in this way? Which stories and passages have been particularly important for you?

10. Which other stories or passages from the Bible would you most like to see reclaimed and reinterpreted for your own life and the lives of other LGBIQ+ people of faith?

11. Which parts of this six-lecture course have touched your life most deeply? Why? How might you bring the lessons you have learned and the insights you have gained into your daily life as an LGBTIQ+ Christian?

12. What now? How can you and your community nurture and deepen your spiritual journeys and share your wisdom and insight with other LGBTIQ+ people and other churches and communities?

Ingram Content Group UK Ltd.
Milton Keynes UK
UKHW040719170423
420292UK00004B/293